ON THE DICTION OF
TENNYSON, BROWNING
AND ARNOLD

S. P. E.
TRACT NO. LIII

ON THE DICTION OF TENNYSON, BROWNING AND ARNOLD

Bernard Groom

ARCHON BOOKS
1970

ORIGINALLY S.P.E. TRACT NO. LIII
PP. 93-147
FIRST PUBLISHED 1939
THE CLARENDON PRESS
REPRINTED 1970 WITH PERMISSION
IN AN UNALTERED AND UNABRIDGED EDITION

ISBN: 0-208-01027-0
PRINTED IN THE UNITED STATES OF AMERICA

ON THE DICTION OF TENNYSON, BROWNING, AND ARNOLD

THE title of a paper in which the names of Tennyson, Browning, and Matthew Arnold are joined together may perhaps recall the famous essay of Walter Bagehot on two of these same poets and the master of the third. Bagehot chose his writers as representatives of three styles: Wordsworth of the Pure, Tennyson of the Ornate, and Browning of the Grotesque. In surveying the language of the three poets who are the subject of this Essay, I was inclined at one time to associate Tennyson, Browning, and Arnold with three epithets applied to different kinds of Poetic Diction—the Traditional, the Eccentric, and the Classical. Further consideration showed that these terms are far too narrow to cover the varieties of style in the three poets under review. Still, at the outset of this complex study, some sort of program is an advantage, and it has become more and more plain to me that in the matter of diction, Tennyson is the skilled professional poet, and in comparison the other two are more or less successful amateurs. Even this general description may be modified in the sequel, though not, I think, to the disadvantage of Tennyson. He is not, as some critics of about forty years ago imagined, 'armed cap-à-pie against criticism'; yet a scrutiny of his language leads to an ever-deepening admiration of his resource and dexterity. How far his eminence in one branch of the poet's art helps to determine his rank among English poets is not a question which comes within the scope of this Essay; yet it is only fair to remark that had Coleridge applied to Tennyson the complaint which he made against Tennyson's chief prototype in classical poetry, 'If you take from Virgil his diction and metre, what do you leave him?' the criticism would have been scarcely more unjust to the English poet than it is to the Roman.

As any discussion of Poetic Diction is critical as well as philological, some mention of critical values is necessary at this point. The notion that poetry should have a language of its own, different in many or even in any respects from that of ordinary life, has often been attacked and is, in some quarters, being attacked now. Applied to a test case, the question is whether the audacious and figurative language which Shakespeare used when at the zenith of his powers is a merit or a defect. Dryden, apparently, considered it a defect, or, at least, as 'too much of a good thing', and, if I understand them aright, some modern critics would agree with him. But against this view is ranged a formidable consensus of opinion. Aristotle, in the *Poetics*, implies that a style alive with metaphors and figures is a distinguishing mark of good poetry, and most of our own critics would agree with Gray that Shakespeare's language is one of his principal beauties, since in him 'every word is a picture'. Coleridge, Lamb, De Quincey, and Hazlitt would have assented with fervour; Arnold would have assented, but with reserve. Though the romantic critics have been justly blamed for creating the myth of Shakespeare's perfection, they have surely done literature a permanent service by maintaining Shakespeare's bold and creative handling of language to be a manifestation of the highest poetic power. They declared his language to be the fit expression of his own imagination and passion; from which view no critic can dissent, whatever he may think of Shakespeare's example to other writers and of his influence upon the language.

But the gifts of the Muses are manifold, and though Shakespeare's example has exercised a strong influence on some of our poets, on others it has been almost negligible. It appears that, in point of style, poets may be divided into two main classes: those who believe that first thoughts are best, and those who hold that retouching is a part of inspiration. To put it differently, there are the impulsive poets, and there are the deliberate poets. No doubt it is really a question of proportion, as all poets are impulsive in some measure and deliberate in some measure: still, the distinction which includes Shakespeare among the poets who never blotted a line and Virgil among those who were content to spend the whole day in polishing a short passage points to a real cleavage of temperament and method. To some poets, perfection is the ideal, others are content with the exhibition of power. The language of Shakespeare has at times the dazzling force of lightning ;

some styles are designed rather for permanence. To this second class belongs Milton, assuredly a 'deliberate' rather than an 'impulsive' poet; and Milton's diction is considered by Professor Wyld, whose opinion commands the greatest respect, to be surpassed by that of no other English poet.[1] This praise, I understand, rests on the view that Milton has a fine sense of the aristocracy of words: he used 'the best words in the best order'—best by their associations and form, and their worthiness to be permanent in the language. The contrast between the Shakespearian and the Miltonic ideals of style is reflected in the work of various groups of minor poets and has presented problems to major ones. During the eighteenth century the influence of Milton was in the ascendant; during the nineteenth century, the freedom and daring of Shakespeare were increasingly admired. In a discussion of diction, therefore, it is impossible to speak as if there were an absolute standard of excellence: the qualities which Shakespeare at his best represents, and the qualities represented by Milton are both, in different ways, admirable. But there is another point. We are often inclined to associate a particular style with a particular writer, forgetting that there is an appropriate style to each form of poetry. Poets have often remembered this better than critics, and have varied their style with the type of poem. It is right that shades of diction no less than forms of metre should distinguish epic from drama, satire from idyll, narrative from description: failure to make good this distinction has been the ruin of many attempts. And there is one further reason why an absolute standard in judging diction is unattainable: the poet and the lexicographer cannot regard words from the same point of view, unless indeed the poet is, like Ben Jonson, a lexicographer at heart, and is disposed to condemn a highly poetic diction as 'no language'. Ordinarily the philologist will prefer the diction which, like Milton's, respects the traditions of the language to one which, like Shakespeare's, subordinates all to the needs of passionate and intense expression. It is, in my opinion, the task of the critic to hold the balance between these conflicting

[1] Henry Cecil Wyld, *Some Aspects of the Diction of English Poetry*, p. 23.

claims. The diction of every poet has its individual features without which its very life would disappear; but the words of the poet are an organic part of the language as a whole, either assisting or injuring its health; and thirdly, there is a fitness of diction for each type or kind of poem. Abundant material for illustrating all these points is supplied by the three poets who are the subject of this paper.

TENNYSON

I

THOUGH Arnold was born thirteen years after Tennyson, and ten after Browning, all three poets belonged to the same generation and shared the same advantages which the age could bestow on its poets. Keen dispute had been held about the diction of poetry by some of the writers of the previous generation, and the matter was still of vital interest to many of their successors. The position of the Victorian was not quite so enviable as that of the Elizabethan. In the matter of diction, the liberty of the Elizabethan poet was unlimited, for hardly any words were felt to be unpoetic. The liberty of the young Victorian poet was somewhat narrower, for Wordsworth's view that there is no essential difference between the language of prose and that of poetry had been generally rejected. On the other hand, the notion that a limited body of 'poetic diction' had a special prestige had been completely exploded. All good poetry of the past was a quarry from which the modern poet might borrow the fitting word: Coleridge and Scott, Shelley and Keats had each discovered from his own reading new sources of verbal wealth. The generation to which Tennyson belonged had not the revolutionary ardour of its predecessor. Many of its members, like Tennyson himself, rated order as high as freedom, and had, like Tennyson, a taste for precision in poetry; there was less of that passionate originality so highly prized in the generation of Wordsworth. On the other hand, Tennyson had no intention of allowing any source of poetic enrichment to be closed to him. He read widely not only in English poetry but in Greek, Latin, and Italian. Like Milton he nourished his own diction from the best sources, native and foreign, thereby forming and strengthening the originality of his style.

II

There were no profound changes in Tennyson's diction during the course of his long poetic career. It is true that in the *Poems* of 1830 the style is not mature, its

elements being imperfectly blended, and it is also true
that the poet adapted his style for particular purposes;
there are, for instance, certain differences in the diction of
the dramas as compared with that of the idylls. None the
less, Tennyson attained a characteristic style early in his
career and he never lost it; in language, at least, the child
was father of the man. Naturally there was some change
and development in the course of so long a life, but much
less than in that of some other poets; no poems of
Tennyson, for instance, differ in diction one quarter as
much as *Michael* and *Laodamia*. One might illustrate the
essentials of Tennyson's diction from the 1842 volume
alone.

To judge from his practice, Tennyson would have
agreed with Gray that the language of poetry is never the
language of the age. He would never have declared his
diction to be founded on the real language of men. It is
palpably the product of art: this is a quality which is
common to all his poems. There are of course varieties.
There is far less visible artifice in the shorter lyrics than
in the *Idylls of the King*; the diction of the impassioned
parts of *Maud* is much simpler than that of *The Princess*.
At rare moments, as in the lines ' Break, break, break ',
Tennyson speaks to the reader's heart in words of perfect
simplicity. But this is not his characteristic manner. His
general attitude is not that of a man speaking to men,
nor is he on quite easy terms with contemporary life.
Some of his poems, like *The Lady of Shalott*, belong to
the world of faery; some are on medieval themes; some
are idylls of more or less artificial simplicity; some, like
In Memoriam, are profoundly meditated and demand a
vocabulary drawn from various sources. To such a poet,
the use of rare and archaic words was a necessity, and in
many of his poems they play an important and calculated
part. In his very early work he values them for their own
sake. *Marish*, for instance, is an old word which has
struck his fancy: he used it, together with *marish-flowers*
in *The Dying Swan*, and *marish-mosses* occurs in *Mariana*.
Lowlihead (*Isabel*) and *eglatere* (*A Dirge*) are other examples
of this kind of diction. As Tennyson's art matured, his
taste for old and rare words grew more discriminating; in
the *Poems* of 1842 and after, the flavour of antiquity, if

introduced at all, is often varied to suit the occasion.
In *St. Simeon Stylites,* for instance, the archaisms have an
appropriate Biblical cast: e.g. *the meed of saints, sawn in
twain, spake, halt and maimed, smite . . . spare not. The
Idylls of the King* are full of archaisms: *Morte d'Arthur,*
for instance, naturally contains echoes of Malory, e.g.
lightly bring me word, lief and dear, slay thee with my hands.
In the later *Idylls* the archaism is less successful. Old
and rare words are used which carry no distinct associations
with them; instead of adding colour to the style, they
give it an air of spurious antiquity. Expressions like the
following are frequent: ' the *foughten* field ',[1] ' *holp* me at
my need ',[2] ' Heaven *yield* her for it ',[3] ' the little *fowl* '[4]
(birds), ' *delivering doom* '[5] (i.e. pronouncing judgement),
' a *grimly* light ',[6] ' many a costly *cate* ',[7] ' this *frontless*
kitchen-knave ',[8] ' for *housel* or for shrift ',[9] ' *approven*
King ',[10] ' *rathe* she rose ',[11] ' sweetly could she *make* and
sing ',[12] ' there was *dole* in Astolat '.[13] The effect of these
phrases in their context may be fairly illustrated from the
following passage, in which the diction, instead of being
poetic, is no more than vaguely ' old ' :

> and he,
> That did not shun to smite me in worse way,
> Had yet that grace of courtesy in him left
> He spared to lift his hand against the King
> Who made him knight: but many a knight was slain;
> And many more, and all his kith and kin
> Clave to him, and abode in his own land.[14]

This tissue of archaic phrases illustrates in an extreme
form the poet's avoidance of ordinary language. At the
outset of this Essay I have mentioned one of the least
successful aspects of Tennyson's style, but I do not mean
to disparage his occasional use of old or rare words, with
more or less poetic associations, like *matin* for ' morning ',
sallow for ' willow ', *herb* for ' grass '. In the greater
part of his work, his use of these variants is eminently
skilful.

[1] *The Coming of Arthur.*   [2] Ibid.
[3] *Gareth and Lynette.*   [4] Ibid.   [5] Ibid.
[6] Ibid.   [7] Ibid.   [8] Ibid.   [9] *Guinevere.*   [10] Ibid.
[11] *Elaine.*   [12] Ibid.   [13] Ibid.   [14] *Guinevere.*

III

We pass naturally from the consideration of Tennyson's old and rare words to a feature of his style which is more peculiar to himself. Many English poets use fanciful and witty expressions which offer a slight puzzle to the reader. Tennyson keeps his reader's mind active by the use of somewhat enigmatic words which not infrequently require explanation. Sometimes the poet solves the difficulty by a note of his own. He tells us, for instance, that the word *balm-cricket* (i.e. cicala), which occurs in his early poem *A Dirge*, is taken from a note on the word τέττιξ by Dalzel, an editor of Theocritus. He also explains that the *redcap* of *The Gardener's Daughter* is a 'goldfinch'. But he does not remove every difficulty, and he has left certain problems to the Editors of the *Oxford Dictionary*. They explain the 'budded *quicks*' of *In Memoriam* as 'probably hawthorn', and comment on 'her clear *germander* eye' (*Sea Dreams*) as referring 'to the beautiful colour of the flowers of *Veronica Chamædrys*'. Some out-of-the-way words present no difficulty, and are simply a form of that graceful artifice of which Tennyson is a master. That most artificial of his poems, *The Princess*, abounds in far-fetched expressions: '*bosks* of wilderness', 'a long low *sibilation*', '*linden* alley', 'we . . . *perused the matting*', 'not in this *frequence*', 'free *adit*', and the like, and sometimes the artifice stands self-confessed, as when, describing the upbringing of two girl friends, the poet writes:

> They were still together, grew,
> (For so they said themselves) inosculated.

Once at least Tennyson somewhat clarified his phrasing in a later edition: the heroine of *The Brook*, on migrating to Australasia, was originally said to breathe 'in converse seasons'; this afterwards became 'breathes in April-autumns'. No feature of Tennyson's language is easier to illustrate than this deliberate and often learned artifice of phrasing, but I will limit myself to a few further examples out of the scores which might be quoted: 'cherish my *prone* year' (*Gareth and Lynette*), *glamour* for 'magic' (ibid.), *delivering* for 'announcing' (ibid.); 'She lived a *moon*

in that low lodge with him' (*Last Tournament*), 'the watch-
men peal The *sliding season*' (*The Gardener's Daughter*),
waning for 'fading' (ibid.), 'the fount of *fictive* tears' (*The
Brook*), 'rust or *soilure*' (*Elaine*), *sequel of guerdon* (*Œnone*).
It would be a mistake to call these recherché expressions
affected, for they are nearly always felicitous, and from
Tennyson, whose mind was the reverse of simple, they
come quite naturally.   Moreover, he does not take himself
so seriously as some of his critics imagine: a poem like
Amphion shows with how slight a manipulation he could
turn his usual style to a comic purpose.

A characteristic of Tennyson's style, somewhat akin to
his use of the far-fetched word, is his use of periphrasis.
This is a familiar feature of poetic diction, and though it
is overdone in the false style denounced in Wordsworth's
Preface, fit occasions for its use often arise.   Tennyson's
periphrases are very various, some being pleasantly fanciful, some playful, a few rather commonplace or even
ridiculous, and some exquisitely beautiful.   Some of his
phrases are merely allusive or slightly decorative, e.g. 'him
that died of hemlock' (*The Princess*), 'the girls all kiss'd
Beneath the sacred bush' (*The Epic*).   The phrase 'bristled
grunters' in *The Princess* agrees with the mock-heroic tone
of that poem, so does the playful description of a Chinese
puzzle:

> Laborious orient ivory sphere in sphere.

Some of the periphrases are, like much of Tennyson's
language, over-elaborate; for instance, the lines in *In
Memoriam*:

> Or where the kneeling hamlet drains
> The chalice of the grapes of God,[1]

may make the reader pause a moment before he recognizes
the allusion to the Sacrament.   But the lines are redeemed
by that rightness of tone which Tennyson always commands when he touches a solemn subject; it recurs in the
passage on Mary, the sister of Lazarus:

> her ardent gaze
> Roves from the living brother's face,
> And rests upon the Life indeed;[2]

[1] Section x.   [2] Section xxxii.

and by the side of, or above, these examples, deserves to be
set the exquisite periphrasis on the life of Jesus:

> the sinless years
> That breathed beneath the Syrian blue.[1]

Equally impressive is 'the silent Opener of the Gate' of
the late poem, *God and the Universe*. Tennyson often
employs periphrasis for natural description: in *Morte
d'Arthur*, icebergs are named 'moving isles of winter', and
the Aurora Borealis is 'the northern morn'. He calls the
dandelion, in a delightful phrase,

> the flower,
> That blows a globe of after arrowlets,[2]

and equally beautiful is his description of the kingfisher
as 'the sea-blue bird of March'.[3] Some of Tennyson's periphrases, after the manner of the eighteenth-century poets,
neatly fill a single line, e.g.

> A lidless watcher of the public weal   (*The Princess*),

and sometimes, in the periphrastic manner imitated from
Milton, an abstract is substituted for a concrete noun, e.g.

> Led on the gray-hair'd wisdom of the east   (*Holy Grail*)
> And all the pavement stream'd with massacre
>   (*Last Tournament*).

Periphrasis may be a powerful weapon in satire, but the
description of a preacher put into the mouth of the hero of
Maud, 'This broad-brimm'd hawker of holy things', does
not strike very hard. Occasionally there is an elaboration
of language which seems uncalled for, as when a beard is
called 'the knightly growth that fringed his lips'.[4] Some
of Tennyson's periphrases seem to indicate a Victorian
shyness to call things by their right names; the birth of
children is a special occasion for this reticence. In *The
Marriage of Geraint*, for instance, an anticipated baby is
called

> another gift of the high God,
> Which, maybe, shall have learn'd to lisp you thanks,

and in *The Miller's Daughter* the birth and untimely death
of a child are veiled in language of great mystery:

[1] *In Memoriam*, lii.   [2] *Gareth and Lynette*.
[3] *In Memoriam*, xci.   [4] *Morte d'Arthur*.

The still affection of the heart
Became an outward breathing type,
That into stillness past again.

For Tennyson periphrasis is often a form of euphemism, and few of his readers can have failed to notice how often he affects the euphemism *pass* for ' die '.

If Tennyson's periphrases sometimes resemble the manner of eighteenth-century verse, his occasional transference or adaptation of the parts of speech connects him with Keats and other writers who adopted that licence from Elizabethan English. Like Keats, Tennyson seldom or never uses the device for the evasion of difficulties, but to produce effects not otherwise attainable. His words in this class are mostly verbs, adapted for the occasion from adjectives or nouns. He is fond of the ' verb ' *gloom*:

twilight *gloom'd* (*The Princess*),

The wan day
Went *glooming* down (*Last Tournament*),

May her life . . . be never *gloom'd* by the curse (*The Wreck*).

The transitive use of *tumble* enables him to form some expressive phrases, e.g. ' *tumbled* fruit ' (*The Princess*), ' fragments *tumbled* from the glens ' (*Œnone*), ' Among the *tumbled* fragments of the hills ' (*Elaine*). The verb ' to orb ' is something of a favourite. ' Tennyson ', says Mr. A. M. D. Hughes, ' frequently uses the words to " round " or to " orb " of a star coming full face; as in " orb into the perfect star ",[1] " all that orbs Between the Northern and the Southern morn " '.[2] Other Tennysonian ' verbs ' are *voice* (*Lucretius*), *tongue* (*Tiresias*), *guerdon* (*The Princess*), *wann'd* (*Maud*).

The transference of the parts of speech is one of Tennyson's means of enriching his poetic vocabulary. Another device which he employs produces an effect like that of his recherché words—it widens the gulf between verse and prose, and is sometimes an aid to euphony. This device is the use of rare forms or spellings of words, e.g. *thridding* for ' threading ', *knolling* for ' knelling ', *scymetar* for ' scimitar '. His care for euphony appears in his preference for the form *Genovese* to ' Genoese ', but his use of *Ithacensian*

---

[1] *In Memoriam*, xxiv.　　　　[2] *The Princess*, v.

for 'Ithacan' is part of that display of rare language by which he enlivens the fantastic theme of *The Princess*. Tennyson makes full though not excessive use of those advantages which arise from a language not strictly standardized, and the use of verse in itself aids the relaxation of usage.   Unlike Browning, he is seldom eccentric, never reckless, though in his early poem *The Merman* there is the form *almondine*, which is an error for 'almandine'. As a rule, his departures from custom either have good precedent, or are of so slight a nature as to be admissible. He uses, on occasion, *lissome* for 'lissom', *landskip* for 'landscape', *harken* for 'hearken', *holly-hoaks* for 'holly-hocks', *plowman* for 'ploughman', *graff* for 'graft', *turkis* (Milton's form) for 'turquoise', and *hern* for 'heron'.   He frequently uses the more phonetic *-t* instead of the *-ed* form of the preterite and participle, as in *dipt, dropt, past, slipt*.[1]   Occasionally his accentuation of words is unusual or archaic, e.g. balúster, retínue,[2] chiválric.[3]   The form *glode* as the preterite of 'glide' in *The Battle of Brunanburh* is, in the phrase of the *Oxford Dictionary*, 'distinctly archaistic'.

IV

So far I have dealt with Tennyson's devices for giving his language the distinction which the use of metre demands.   These devices do not, as in some poets, contrast strongly with the rest of his language, for Tennyson is far too skilful to be the dupe rather than the master of any device which he chooses to employ.   He turns what might be and often has been a fettering convention into a means of displaying the resources of the English language and of his own art.   It remains to consider those aspects of his diction in which he is writing more creatively; and naturally his language is most poetic when he is free to achieve effects of his own choice, and is not simply using an alternative expression in order to avoid a commonplace equivalent.   But there is also an intermediate phase of his

---

[1] Cf. also, 'knōwledge, shōne, knōll—let him who reads me always read the vowel on these words long' (Tennyson, *Author's Prefatory Notes.*)

[2] 'The usual stressing in the 16th–18th centuries' (*O.E.D.*).

[3] 'The pronunciation sanctioned by the poets' (ibid.).

work which calls for notice, namely, his endeavour to adapt the art of poetry to the needs of contemporary life and thought, a task involving the use of many expressions not previously associated with verse. Whatever our view of Tennyson as an original thinker, it is certain that he kept well abreast of the new movements in thought during his century, and he reflects the impact of those thoughts on the mind of his generation more clearly and completely than any other writer. During his life, the sciences gained much of that eminence in the intellectual world which they now possess, and Tennyson's position as Poet Laureate was a challenge to him to illustrate the truth of what Wordsworth had written in his Preface to the *Lyrical Ballads*: 'If the labours of Men of science should ever create any material revolution, direct or indirect, in our condition, and in the impressions which we habitually receive, the Poet will sleep then no more than at present; he will be ready to follow the steps of the Man of science, not only in those general indirect effects, but he will be at his side, carrying sensation into the midst of the objects of the science itself.'

That Tennyson met the situation with such success is a striking testimony to his mastery of language, though that success was perhaps due in part to his limitation as a thinker, or at least to his prudence as a poet. In his more serious verse, he deals only with broad scientific conceptions, the names of which are mostly simple, and cause his verse little embarrassment. There is no incongruity in the use of such language in this stanza from *In Memoriam*:

> Are God and Nature then at strife,
> That Nature lends such evil dreams?
> So careful of the *type* she seems,
> So careless of the single life,[1]

or in *Lucretius*:

> Vanishing, *atom and void, atom and void,*
> Into the unseen for ever.

In his lighter moods, he delights in the technical problems presented him by uncouth names, and displays his skill in weaving them dexterously into the fabric of his verse. In *The Princess* is a well-known geological passage on the 'stony names'

[1] Section lv.

> Of shale and hornblende, rag and trap and tuff,
> Amygdaloid and trachyte,

also a mathematical line:

> Of sine and arc, spheroïd and azimuth,

and in *Merlin and Vivien* is a learned conversation on falconry and its terms of art,

> Diet and seeling, jesses, leash and lure.

Some of the new scientific words are rendered attractive to him by their sonorous syllables, like *mastodon*,[1] or a botanical name will be interwoven into an alliterative line,

> Sweeping the froth-fly from the fescue;[2]

and though he poetizes an allusion to clockwork machinery as 'every kiss of toothed wheels ',[3] he does not shun such terms of industrial progress as *trucks* and *trams*,[4] or of finance as 'dividend, consol, and share '.[5]   In one and the same poem (*Aylmer's Field*), he will use a plain colloquialism like 'Call'd to the bar ', and also summon up his powers of verbal elaboration to describe 'the lawless science of our Law ':

> That codeless myriad of precedent,
> That wilderness of single instances.

I doubt whether full justice has been done to the skill with which Tennyson reconciles the traditions of poetry with the new terms which were current in his lifetime among the Victorian clerisy.

V

Like most of our chief poets since Spenser, Tennyson enriches his language with various words in which certain affixes have been used to form new compounds.   It is sometimes difficult to determine whether the poet has himself formed such compounds, or has borrowed them from some little-known passage of an earlier date, but as a rule the distinction is without importance.   Tennyson is too careful to overdo the use of any one affix, though like most writers he has his preferences.   The prefix *dis-* is something of a favourite: he uses, for instance, the new or rare compounds *dislink, dishelm, discage, disprince, dis-*

[1] *The Epic.*   [2] *Aylmer's Field.*
[3] *In Memoriam*, cxvii.   [4] *Maud*, x. i.   [5] *The Wreck.*

edge, disroot. He also makes some use of the prefixes *in-* and *en-*, as in *inswathe, immantle, encarnalize, empanoply, ensepulchre,* also of the suffix *-ful,* as in *spleenful* (used by Keats), *mightful, prideful, gustful*; and like Carlyle he employs the suffix *-ism* for denunciatory or contemptuous formations such as *animalism, babyism, antibabylonianism* : *kitchendom* too is in Carlyle's manner. The somewhat rare prefix *counter-* appears as the first element in several compounds, e.g. *counterchange, countercharm, counterpressure,* and *counter motion.*[1] Like many Victorian poets he has a taste for compound adverbs beginning with *a-,* e.g. *adown, anear, agrin, anight,* the first two of which were familiar in verse before Tennyson's time.

The use of common or familiar words is perhaps the best touchstone of an English poet's mastery of language. The subject involves some consideration of style as well as of diction in the narrower sense, for familiar words cannot be used effectively unless there is some exertion of the poet's higher powers. As often as not, the common elements of language owe their greater significance in poetry to an element, latent or revealed, of metaphor. To omit this part of my subject on the ground that it belongs more properly to literary criticism would, I think, injure the value of the discussion : I shall, therefore, deal with Tennyson's use of common and familiar words as a feature of his poetic style, as well as of his ' diction ' in the more philological sense of the word.

In the *Memoir* of his father, Lord Tennyson quotes a letter written to the poet by a Lancashire miner, Samuel Bamford. It ends with a few words of naïve but excellent criticism: 'But your English ! why it is almost unlimitedly expressive. This language of ours, what can it not be made to say ? What height, what depth filled with all glorious hues, terrible glooms, and vivid flashes does it not combine and your poems exhibit all.' Tennyson is, indeed, wonderfully effective in his use of the fundamental words in our vocabulary; that is, words of Anglo-Saxon origin, old-established and fully naturalized words from Norse and French sources, and certain words of obscure or popular origin which are first recorded about 1200—

---

[1] Printed as two words.

1400 and are often peculiarly expressive. These groups of words form the foundation of our language, and Tennyson is the master of every device by which they can be made to strike home with special force. Sometimes the effect is produced by the apt placing of words in a particular context, as in the simple sentence, ' The slow clock ticking', in *Mariana*. Sometimes it is done by metaphor, as in that phrase from *The Lady of Shalott* which was derisively italicized by the *Quarterly* reviewer:

> On either side the river lie
> Long fields of barley and of rye,
> That clothe the wold and *meet the sky*;

sometimes by metaphor aided by metrical manipulation, as in the last line of a section of *In Memoriam*:

> He is not here; but far away
> The noise of life begins again,
> And ghastly thro' the drizzling rain
> *On the bald street breaks the blank day*[1]

All readers who, in the excellent phrase of Walter Raleigh, admire Tennyson because they are fond of beautiful language, may probably find in these three quotations the types of many of their favourite passages. Occasionally it seems his deliberate purpose to illustrate the wealth of English in popular expressive verbs:

> The parrot scream'd, the peacock *squall'd* . . .
> The palace *bang'd* and *buzz'd* and *clackt*.[2]

With a fuller exercise of his skill he will so choose a particular verb that it gives life to a whole sentence, and in return receives life from it. Like other writers of the time, e.g. Ruskin, he is fond of producing this effect by verbs of motion, using them metaphorically in descriptions to suggest an imaginary or to emphasize an actual movement, as in:

> The narrow street that *clamber'd* toward the mill.[3]

> The maiden splendours of the morning star
> *Shook* in the steadfast blue.[4]

> The long light *shakes* across the lakes.[5]

[1] Section vii.
[2] *The Day-Dream : The Revival.*
[3] *Enoch Arden.*
[4] *Dream of Fair Women.*
[5] *The Princess*, iv.

The landscape *winking* through the heat.[1]

He produces many vivid effects from the metaphorical use of verbs associated with 'burning', e.g.

> The helmet and the helmet-feather
> *Burn'd* like one *burning* flame together.[2]

> Unloved, that beech will gather brown,
> This maple *burn* itself away.[3]

> The light cloud *smoulders* on the summer crag [4]

> The furzy prickle *fire* the dells [5]

> Its stormy crests that *smoke* against the skies [6]

And in many passages, which are surely the pride of every poet who can produce them, he makes us feel—by a delicate fitness of words to a particular purpose—that familiar language is charged with a new potency of expression. This effect is produced, for instance, in:

> A still salt pool, lock'd in with bars of sand,
> Left on the shore; that hears all night
> The *plunging seas* draw backward from the land
> Their moon-led waters white.[7]

> The chestnut *pattering* to the ground.[8]

> The rooks are *blown about* the skies.[9]

But this quality cannot be fairly illustrated from a few quotations, for in varying degrees it pervades the whole of Tennyson's work.

A close study of Tennyson's diction shows us that in him, as in most essentially poetic natures, language is inseparably blended with thought and sensation. It is often impossible to say whether the expression suggests the idea or the idea the expression, whether the sensation prompts the word, or the word stimulates the sensation. The interaction of feeling and language in Tennyson's mind may be illustrated by the following passage in *Lancelot and Elaine*:

> the blood-red light of dawn
> Flared in her face, she *shrilling*, 'Let me die!'

[1] *In Memoriam*, lxxxix.   [2] *Lady of Shalott*.
[3] *In Memoriam*, ci.   [4] *Edward Morris*.   [5] *Two Voices*.
[6] *Lancelot and Elaine*.   [7] *Palace of Art*.
[8] *In Memoriam*, xi.   [9] Ibid. xv.

The reader may naturally consider that this unusual verb
was chosen to suggest a particular cry, partly pathetic,
partly hysterical; and this in a way is true.   Yet it appears
also that 'shrill' was, for Tennyson, a useful but inde-
terminate verb capable of suggesting different sounds
in different contexts ; and we can therefore hardly doubt
that the possession of such a verb played some part in
creating the occasions for its use.   In *The Holy Grail* the
verb ' shrill' is used of the loud insistent cry of a man, in
Gareth and Lynette of a woman's voice raised in petu-
lance and contempt, in *The Last Tournament* of the excited
voice of a Court Fool, and in *Merlin and Vivien* of a
falcon's bells; and in each passage the verb seems peculiarly fitted to the occasion.   The discovery and possession
of words which will take on various shades of meaning is
not only a powerful aid to a poet, it may be one of the
impulses which prompt his invention.   For Tennyson, a
significant phrase was sometimes the nucleus of an entire
poem. A sentence in *The Times*, 'Some one had blundered ',[1]
was the germ of his *Charge of the Light Brigade*; the
words of a dying man, ' God Almighty little knows what
He's about taking me ', were the occasion of *Northern
Farmer, Old Style*; the phrase 'too late' clearly suggested
the maiden's song in *Guinevere*, and the words *Frater ave
atque vale* are the motive of the poem so entitled.   The
lines *Far-far-away*, written in Tennyson's old age, are
built upon the title-phrase, words which, as the poet tells
us, stirred in his boyhood what can only be called a ' cosmic
emotion ' :

> What vague world-whisper, mystic pain or joy,
> Thro' those three words would haunt him when a boy,
>   Far-far-away?

Just as phrases are often the germ of poems, so words are
often the germ of phrases, images, and poetic ideas.   There
is a wonderful continuity and connectedness of diction
in Tennyson's work, and often the full poetic beauty of
certain words is only apparent when they are illustrated
by the same words in other passages.   I do not undertake
to supply a full list of Tennyson's favourite and characteristic words—the germ of much of his loveliest writing

[1] *Tennyson: A Memoir*, i. 381.

—but such a list would certainly include *glimmer, moan,
verge, slope, gloom, windy, myriad, hollow, dip, flicker, crisp,
droop, fret, level.*[1] These are not all used very often, but
they are many times the central·words in passages of
especial charm or beauty. To these must be added various
verbs beginning with *sl-*, like the three which occur in one
of the lyrics of *The Princess*:

> Now *sleeps* the crimson petal, now the white . . .
> Now *slides* the silent meteor on . . .
> Now folds the lily all her sweetness up,
> And *slips* into the bosom of the lake;

but the favourites of this group are *slope* and *slant*. On
the significance of many of these words, especially perhaps
slope and *glimmer*, much might be written, but I will con-
fine myself to the special interest attaching to the group
moan, boundless, deep. Tennyson was a great sea-poet, and
these three words seem to have dwelt in his mind in his
broodings on the sea, slowly accumulating suggestiveness
and meaning during the whole of his life. The culmination
is reached in *Crossing the Bar*. In phrases from earlier
poems one may watch the poet moving tentatively towards
some unknown goal:

> The deep
> Moans round with many voices.   (*Ulysses*)

And I from out the boundless outer deep . . . (*Sea Dreams*)

And the low moan of leaden-colour'd seas . . .   (*Enoch Arden*)

> But that one ripple on the boundless deep . . .
> (*The Ancient Sage*)

Each of these passages is good in itself; yet all that is
hidden in the three words is not fully revealed until that
last sea-piece in which the poet prays that there may be
'no moaning of the bar':

> When that which drew from out the boundless deep
> Turns again home.

It was justly said by Tennyson's son, when he first read
Crossing the Bar, ' That is the crown of your life's work.'

[1] On 'verbal inspiration' in this sense of the term, see my article
Some Kinds of Poetic Diction (pp. 153 and seqq.) (Essays and Studies
of the English Association, vol. xv).

V

To the end of his days Tennyson was an active reader of the Greek and Roman classics, and he had in general no prejudice in favour of a non-literary or non-learned style. But he belonged to a generation which had been taught by Wordsworth to appreciate the beauty of simplicity. In some of his idylls he attempts a manner which is not natural to him, and Arnold rightly contrasts the 'semblance of simplicity' of a poem like *Dora* with the 'real simplicity' of a poem like *Michael*. Tennyson's natural style is an eclectic one, a fabric woven of many colours. It is a blending of originality and conservatism, of invention and scholarship. He does not offer learning as a substitute for poetry. In *Ulysses* there are Homeric echoes—*barren crags* (κραναὴ 'Ιθάκη), *windy Troy* ("Ιλιος ἠνεμόεσσα), *sitting well in order, smite The sounding furrows* (ἑξῆς δ' ἑζόμενοι πολιὴν ἅλα τύπτον ἐρετμοῖς)—but the general tone is far from being coldly classical. Equally far is *Morte d'Arthur* from being narrowly medieval: the Virgilian line

This way and that dividing the swift mind

shows that the author's love of literary elaboration is not to be sacrificed to a pedantic doctrine of propriety. Nor are reminiscences of Greek poetry confined to poems on Greek subjects. The epithet *deep-meadow'd*, for instance, also in *Morte d'Arthur*, is from Pindar's βαθυλείμων. Latinisms in Tennyson's vocabulary are not infrequent, but they are scarcely common enough to constitute a marked feature of his style. He uses *eminent* in the sense of 'projecting',[1] *subjected* in the sense of 'lying beneath',[2] *fable* like the Latin 'fabula',[3] *frequence* for 'crowd',[4] *lucid* in the sense of 'shining'.[5] These are typical among Tennyson's Latinisms, and none are very striking or conspicuous words. Tennyson makes no effort to exclude the traces of classical reading from his ordinary style, but he does not rely on them for any important effect. In brief, the 'classical' features of his diction show both his reading and his complete lack of pedantry.

On his use of compound words, especially of compound epithets, much of the poetic effect of Tennyson's style

---

[1] *Love and Death.*   [2] *Tiresias.*   [3] *The Gardener's Daughter.*
[4] *The Princess.*   [5] e.g. *The Lover's Tale.*

depends. He is not so prolific in his formations as Keats,
nor does he pour such a wealth of imagination into them,
but, with that single exception, no English poet is more
felicitous in his compound words. I have enumerated
elsewhere [1] the traditional types of the compound epithet
in English poetry, and to one or other of these classes
nearly all of Tennyson's formations belong; he is no lover
of the 'asyntactic' type, so much affected by G. M.
Hopkins. His favourite kind is the parasynthetic compound, e.g. ' *crimson-circled* star ',[2] ' *million-myrtled* wilderness ',[3] ' *deep-dimpled* current ',[4] ' *horny-nibb'd* raven ',[5] and
his most beautiful formations are those in which this type
is combined with metaphor, e.g. ' *dewy-tassell'd* wood ',[6]
' *shadowy-pencill'd* vallies ',[7] ' *ruby-budded* lime '.[8]   Another
kind which he often uses is what I have called the bi-
adjectival type, e.g. *human-amorous, wan-sallow, stately-
gentle, silver-misty, divisible-indivisible* (world).   His compound nouns are less frequent but, like the adjectives,
they mostly have some verbal beauty, great or small, and
scarcely one is an example of bare grammatical convenience
or poetic licence.   Specimen compound nouns are : *apple-
arbiter, sea-cataracts, sea-voice, sea-lane, torrent-bow, foam-
bow.*   Some of Tennyson's compounds are in a lighter
vein, e.g. ' a *something-pottle-bodied* boy ',[9] and a few seem
rhetorical rather than poetic, like the phrase ' *giant-factoried*
city-gloom,'[10] but as a rule Tennyson is true to his principle that the licences and conventions of verse must,
whenever used, be justified by some touch of authentic
poetry.

Some other features of Tennyson's diction remain to be
mentioned, but as they do not raise points of much critical
interest, they can be dealt with shortly.   One is his use of
onomatopoeia, whether in single words or in passages.
Much has been written of Tennyson's direct verbal imita-
tion of sounds in passages like that in *Morte d'Arthur* :

> Dry clashed his harness in the icy caves
> And barren chasms,

and it is true that such effects are fairly common.   There

---

[1] *S.P.E. Tract, No. XLIX.*   [2] *In Memoriam*, lxxxix.   [3] *Lucretius.*
[4] *Gareth and Lynette.*   [5] *Battle of Brunanburh.*
[6] *In Memoriam*, lxxxvi.   [7] *The Daisy.*   [8] *Maud*, I. IV. I.
[9] *Will Waterproof's Lyrical Monologue.*   [10] *Sea-Dreams.*

is nothing very wonderful about them, and I agree with
Mr. Geoffrey Tillotson, who in his excellent work *On
the Poetry of Pope* remarks: 'Onomatopoeia is a childish
effect if it is carried to the extent to which, for instance,
Tennyson carried it in the *Idylls*. In his tournaments
Tennyson seems to be expecting to produce the actual
sounds, rather than to suggest them.' But scarcely anything Tennyson wrote is to be taken less seriously than
these tournaments, which are perhaps too well known.
Tennyson has suffered an injustice from the undue emphasis laid by critics, both friendly and hostile, on the
onomatopoeic aspect of his style. How various is his
command of poetic language I have in some measure
already shown, and to speak of him as *par excellence* the
poet of onomatopoeia would be as unjust as to quote
Virgil's line

Quadripedante putrem sonitu quatit ungula campum

as a representative specimen of the style of the *Aeneid*.
Tennyson has many lines of similar quality, like

The sound of many a heavily-galloping hoof,[1]

and he is equally fond of onomatopoeia in short phrases and
single words, but we need not pause long on this 'childish'
characteristic. I have already given insatnces of the vivid
sound-effect which he elicits from familiar words: 'The
tempest crackles on the leads'[2] is an example which may
be set beside 'The chestnut pattering to the ground', and
yet another is the reiteration of the name 'Maud' to imitate
the cawing of rooks: 'Maud, Maud, Maud, Maud, They
were crying and calling.'[3] Tennyson also makes frequent
use of purely onomatopoeic single words, as in '*cheep*
and twitter',[4] 'not a cricket *chirr'd*',[5] 'A thousand wants
Gnarr at the heels of man',[6] and there is also an 'echoic
expressiveness' in 'The wood which *grides* and clangs Its
leafless ribs and iron horns Together'.[7] His well-known
dislike of sibilants (except where a special sound-effect
was required) and his taste for 'hollow oes and aes, deep-
chested music' naturally exerted some influence on his
vocabulary. An illustration of his attention to detail is

---

[1] *Geraint and Enid.*   [2] *Sir Galahad.*   [3] *Maud*, I. xii. i.
[4] *The Princess*, iv.   [5] *In Memoriam*, xcv.   [6] Ibid. xcviii.
[7] Ibid. cvii.

his change of *river's* to *river* in the line: 'They saw the
gleaming river's seaward flow'.[1] Like other masters of
beautiful language, Tennyson had a sense of the music of
proper names, but it is characteristic of his taste that he
indulged this feeling very sparingly. In his earliest verse,
names like Lilian, Madeline, and Oriana are prominent,
sometimes excessively so; in his maturity, a line like

> Clelia, Cornelia, with the Palmyrene [2]

is a rarity. His manipulation of proper names in metre
is always skilful. His poem, *The Daisy*, contains examples
which linger in the memory:

> But when we crost the Lombard plain
> Remember what a plague of rain;
> Of rain at Reggio, rain at Parma;
> At Lodi, rain, Piacenza, rain,

and

> The rich Virgilian rustic measure
> Of Lari Maxume, all the way.

In *Boadicea* he shows with what dexterity he can handle
unwieldy names like *Icenian*, *Catieuchlanian*, and *Prasu-
tagus*.

The language of Tennyson's poems in dialect does not
come within the scope of this Essay, but it is a point of
interest in his general style that he finds use for several
dialectal words in descriptive passages, e.g. 'fast-falling
burns',[3] 'sleeping *tarn*',[4] 'within the dark and dimpled
beck',[5] 'down the shingly *scaur*',[6] 'the bushless *Pike*'.[7]
Tennyson's language is a very extensive subject; there are
certain points which have not been touched upon, and
many illustrations which might have been used have been
omitted. But it is time to turn to his contemporary who,
though he shares the same Victorian background, is in
many ways so strong a contrast.

[1] *The Lotus-Eaters.*   [2] *The Princess*, ii.
[3] *Gareth and Lynette.*   [4] *Pelleas and Ettarre.*
[5] *The Miller's Daughter.*   [6] *Elaine.*   [7] *Ode to Memory.*

BROWNING

I

IT is now fifty years since the death of Browning, and
twenty-five more since the publication of *Dramatis Personae*,
after which time his style underwent a perceptible change.
During his lifetime Browning was a poet for clever people :
at present, he is little read by the clever, though he still
has admirers among the intelligent—those of the intelligent who have discovered that his work repays the labour
of some study. It is certain that much of Browning's
poetry has kept its vitality, and it is unlikely that poetry
written more than half a century ago should be able to do
this solely by its intellectual interest. There was a time
when Browning's cleverest admirers thought principally of
his meaning or 'message', and it was interesting to point
the contrast between Tennyson, the artist, and Browning,
the philosopher. That view is no longer possible. In one
respect at least Browning's technique needs no defence :
Saintsbury's *History of English Prosody* establishes, once and
for all, the high quality of his metrical art. The question
of his language is more difficult. Its faults even in his
best period are undeniable. Browning will never win
admirers by the manifest attractions of his style. On the
other hand, its merits are evident enough for those who
choose to look, and one great merit, that of being 'varied
in discourse' was justly ascribed to Browning in the well-
known lines of Landor. Browning's happy effects are not
the result of mere luck, as has sometimes been suggested.
An analysis of his dramatic monologues shows him to have
possessed the poet's instinct of long self-preparation for
new and original achievement, and many of the features
of his style are, as we shall see, due to the exigencies of
his favourite form. The clue to an understanding of
Browning's technique is to regard his early work as a progress towards, and his later work as a decline from, the art
of the dramatic monologue as he practises it in his best years
—that is, during the period which begins about the time
of his marriage and ends shortly after his wife's death.

Browning, of course, knew that his attitude towards
poetry was unusual. In the last year of his life he wrote

a letter to Professor Knight in which, as his biographer, Mrs. Sutherland Orr, remarks, 'he states the view of the position and function of poetry, in one brief phrase which might form the text to an exhaustive treatise':—'It is certainly the right order of things: Philosophy first, and Poetry, which is its highest outcome, afterward—and much harm has been done by reversing the natural process.' This doctrine is in marked conflict with the theory that words and thought come simultaneously into the mind of the poet, that the poet knows what he wants to express by expressing it. Besides holding this theory of expression, Browning was a confirmed word-collector. As soon as he had chosen poetry as his vocation, he read through Johnson's *Dictionary*, and throughout his career he not only coined words, but adopted and adapted them freely from various languages. He had no fastidious shyness of influences: his inner life was so robust that he delighted to rub shoulders with the outer world—the world of ideas and words, no less than the world of men and women. Hence his work reflects many aspects of the language of his time: it is a magazine of colloquial phrases, it is rich in learned and artistic terms, and it contains no less a wealth of words associated with poetry in general and Victorian poetry in particular. All these aspects of his diction will be noticed in turn; but I will first deal with his use of traditionally 'poetic' words, as it is in this respect that his work offers the most striking and instructive contrast with that of Tennyson.

Although the language of Browning varies much in different poems, some use of 'poetic' words is a fairly constant feature of his style. I imagine that most readers of Browning do not much notice these words: they are not so handled as to be conspicuous. In a few of his poems some traditional diction is almost inevitable. The theme of *Saul*, for instance, with its Biblical atmosphere, impels the author to use various 'poetic' words, and forms of words, in the familiar way: examples are *chaunt, 'gan, upsoareth, 'twixt, 'neath, inconscious, of yore, wot, ope, behest.* Such diction actually occurs in much of Browning's other work, but as often as not it is smothered and buried beneath a weight of alien associations. The following is a short list, which could be easily increased, of 'poetic' words used in different parts of his work: *abysm, aëry, besprent, bosky, burthen, cinct, clomb, drear, dreriment, empery, hests, marge, marish, murk, pens* (feathers), *ope, steed, thrid, syllable* (verb).   None of these words would cause the least surprise if met with in *Endymion* or *Hyperion*, and many of them are used by Tennyson.   But in the effect which they produce the difference is great.   Keats and Tennyson choose them for their atmosphere and associations, but to Browning they are more often than not the merest makeshifts.   *Ope*, for example, occurs again and again; but it is simply a strange monosyllable in a context of ordinary English.   When Tennyson writes:

> The circle widens till it lip the marge,

he gives an unhurried rhythm to the line which invites the reader to savour the words one by one, and the rare concluding word is in harmony with the rest; but when Browning uses the same word in *Instans Tyrannus*:

> Say rather, from marge to blue marge
> The whole sky grew his targe,

he seems to be clipping the final syllable partly in his haste, partly to fit the rhyme.   So, too, in the line:

> Twitch out five *pens* when plucking one would serve,

there is no apparent advantage in the poetic word for 'feathers', except that as a monosyllable it suits the metre. These examples are typical.   Browning rarely uses what the dictionary calls a 'poetic' word to produce a poetic effect.   He shows no more respect to one word than to another; he appears impatient of the finer tones of diction.

The variety of Browning's language is illustrated by his compound words, many of them new, formed by means of affixes.   He has the Victorian taste for compound adverbs of which the first element is the prepositional prefix *a-*, as in *adrift*.   Such words in the verse of the time usually have a romantic grace or charm.   Some of Browning's also have this quality, but a great many are wholly different, being formed in a mood of jest or mockery.   The following is a varied specimen list: *a-bloom, a-blush, a-bubble, a-chuckle, a-clatter, a-crackle, a-crumble, a-flare, a-flaunt, a-flicker, a-flutter, a-glimmer, a-grime, a-heap, a-seethe, a-simmer, a-smoke, a-spread, a-straddle, a-tangle, a-waft, a-whirl, a-wing.* A similarly mixed list might be compiled from the compounds formed with the prefix *be-*, though probably there would be a preponderance of jocular formations. Some affixes naturally lend themselves to a particular tone or style. For instance, Browning's compound verbs beginning with *en-* are mostly serious or romantic; even taken out of their context they suggest something of the pre-Raphaelite flavour, e.g. *enarm, enchase, encircle, enhaloed, enisled, enmesh, enwreathe.* His compounds ending with the suffix *-ry* are, as might be expected, of a very different quality: *archbishopry, cousinry, dupery, enginery, gossipry, serpentry, stitchery, varletry*; perhaps the most serious formation in this group is *artistry*, of which Browning is perhaps the inventor. The use of adjectives ending with the suffix *-some* is characteristic of his style, e.g. *lightsome, toothsome, playsome, pranksome.* Such words agree with his prevailing colloquial tone; so do others of a similar type, e.g. *beseemingness(es), darlingness, uncomfortableness.* Many compounds he uses are rare or obsolescent, e.g. *lathen* (of lath), *griefful, blinkard, plenitudinous, morbify, immerd, dissheathe, celestiality.* Such lists do something to suggest the vast range of the vocabulary which is needed when a mind so rapid, subtle, and original expresses itself in metrical form.

II

To do justice to Browning's style it is necessary to consider the special objects which he had in view. His most finished and elaborate works are the dramatic monologues of his middle period, and though it is of the essence of these poems that each is a highly individual work, yet they possess certain general qualities in common. For one thing, it is part of his plan to devise a situation in which the speaker should be able to unburden his mind with absolute freedom. Several of the speakers even pause to reflect on this frankness. For instance, Karshish in *An Epistle* apologizes for troubling his correspondent with private matters:

> I half resolve to tell thee, yet I blush,
> What set me off a-writing first of all.[1]

[1] *An Epistle*, 65–6.

Bishop Blougram's visitor is one who imposes no restraint
on the tongue of his host:

> Whereas I should not dare for both my ears
> Breathe one such syllable, smile one such smile,
> Before my chaplain who reflects myself—
> My shade's so much more potent than your flesh.[1]

Caliban, at the end of his monologue, laments his indis-
cretion in talking so freely:

> There scuds His raven that has told Him all!
> It was fool's play, this prattling![2]

To suit the frankness of these self-revelations, Browning
cultivates the utmost informality of style. His handling
of colloquial idiom in little pieces like *The Lost Mistress*
and *Confessions* is one of his finest achievements, and he
shows the same skill on a larger scale in the best of the
monologues. The excellence of the colloquial tone in
poems like *Andrea del Sarto, An Epistle, Bishop Blougram's
Apology*, and, one may add, *Cleon*—though there the manner
is more stately—is evident, and equally evident are the
subtle distinctions of style which mark off each poem from
the others.

The mass of Browning's inferior work should not be
allowed to obscure his masterpieces, but it must be admitted that few poets were so little formed by nature to
woo perfection. Having mastered the colloquial style in
verse, it was characteristic of him to go too far and become
too colloquial. He had a bent towards the jocose, the
disparaging, and the satirical, and in his later work he gave
the impulse free play. This, of course, was partly due to
his choice of imperfect and flawed characters as the main
subjects of his poetry; but it was due as well to his own
explosive vigour. His impatient energy impels him to
give a ludicrous turn to the plainest statement. The line

> How both knelt down, prayed blessing on bent head

might have been written by Browning about the time of
his *Pauline*, or he might have composed it when in the
rare mood of *The Guardian-Angel*, but it is much more
like him to write (as in fact he does):

---

[1] *Bishop Blougram's Apology*, 929–32.
[2] *Caliban upon Setebos*, 286–7.

How both *flopped* down, prayed blessing on bent *pate*,[1]

Again, other men might have written the line:

Pitted against a pair of juveniles,

but the version of Browning is, of course:

Pitted against a *brace* of juveniles.[2]

The mood of satire, whether gay or grave, is so common that it colours Browning's whole style: in no other poet of the century is to be found so large a store of contemptuous or disparaging words. Thus besides *pate* for 'head', he finds many occasions for *noddle*; for 'speak' he frequently uses *prate*; for 'bow' he will substitute *lout*; for 'child', *bantling*; for 'move', *budge*; for 'wrath', *bile*; for 'bear' (verb), *spawn*; for 'go' or 'march', *trundle*. 'Daub his phyz' is quite Browningesque, so is 'we drub Self-knowledge rather, into frowzy pate'. He searches out odd words of this abusive class, finding (for instance) *letch*, *chouse*, *shag-rag*, and sometimes he enforces the effect by alliteration, as in the line:

And nuns a-maundering here and mumping there.

Many of these examples have been drawn from Browning's later work: his style has less equilibrium after about 1864, the date of *Dramatis Personae*; but even in *Men and Women*, where his writing is most balanced, the note of exuberant mockery begins to be heard—for instance, in *Holy-Cross Day*.

III

Verbal reminiscences from other poets are fairly common in Browning's work, and though they do not by themselves give a full idea of his style, they suggest what its tendencies are. His early work shows some traces of romantic diction, as in the line:

That under-current soft and *argentine*[3]

where the last word might have been borrowed from Keats; and there is a well-known echo of Keats's manner

[1] *The Ring and the Book*, vi. 378.   [2] Ibid. v. 1356.
[3] *Sordello*.

in the song 'Heap cassia' in *Paracelsus*. Reminiscences of the fine passages in other poets do not disappear from Browning's later writing, but as the dramatic character of his work increases they come to be chosen more and more for a dramatic purpose, like the quotations of Bishop Blougram in his reflections on Shakespeare:

> He leaves his towers and gorgeous palaces
> To build the trimmest house in Stratford town . . .
> Enjoys a show, respects the puppets, too,
> And none more, had he seen its entry once,
> Than 'Pandulph, of fair Milan Cardinal'.[1]

Such references are characteristic of Blougram, but not of his creator. Browning's non-dramatic echoes of other men's words are of a more original type. The tendency towards abuse and disparagement which we noticed before is evident again here. Numberless English writers have shown their familiarity with Shakespeare's language, and Browning is among them, but it is not so much the highways of his poetry which he seems to know, as its bypaths and even its underworld. The phrases which he echoes from *Hamlet* are of this kind: 'to be round with you', 'Provençal roses', 'chop-fallen',[2] 'imposthume',[3] 'squeak and gibber'.[4] From *Othello* he remembers 'clink the cannikin'[5] ('let me the canakin clink'), 'prove a haggard':[6] the phrase 'nor cog nor cozen'[7] is perhaps a variation of 'cogging, cozening slave'. From *Macbeth* he remembers 'lily-livered'.[8] 'Mewls'[9] is presumably from *As You Like It*, and 'clapperclawing'[10] from *The Merry Wives of Windsor*. 'Just-lugged bear'[11] sounds like a variant of 'head-lugged bear' in *King Lear*, and 'treads close on kibe'[12] is Shakespearian, but not from any one passage. From Milton, as might be imagined, he does not borrow much, but one word at least is a highly characteristic choice, viz. *scrannel*.[13] His borrowings from other writers are of a similar type: for instance, he uses Scott's *hellicat* (spelt 'helicat') in *The Flight of the*

---

[1] *Bishop Blougram's Apology*, 513–14, 517–19.
[2] *The Ring and the Book*, vi. 134.   [3] Ibid. vii. 1145.
[4] Ibid. xi. 702–3.   [5] *The Flight of the Duchess*, xvi.
[6] *The Ring and the Book*, v. 710.   [7] *Holy-Cross Day*.
[8] *Ned Bratts*, 86.   [9] *Aristophanes' Apology*.
[10] *Pietro of Albano*, 166.   [11] *Ned Bratts*, 201.
[12] *The Ring and the Book*, x. 1904.   [13] Ibid. vi. 1000.

Duchess (xiii). From Donne, with whom he has some
affinity, he borrows the rare verb *outstreat*.[1] Of Bunyan,
a spiritual fighter like himself, he was a close reader, and
Bunyan provides him with several phrases. The allusion
to Apollyon in *Childe Roland to the Dark Tower Came*[2] is,
of course, from *The Pilgrim's Progress*, and the description
of Christian's fight with Apollyon who 'stradled quite
over the whole breadth of the way' leaves a trace in the
phrase 'a-straddle across its length' in *Ned Bratts*, which
is a poem on two of Bunyan's converts. Browning also
remembers the disdainful phrase bestowed on Faithful in
Vanity Fair: ' "a sorry scrub," said Mr. High-Mind.'
The phrase is repeated in *Aristophanes' Apology*, and 'a
sorry little scrub' occurs in *Fra Lippo Lippi*. To illustrate
Browning's verbal reminiscences I have drawn on only a
few of his poems, but further examples would emphasize
the same points.

IV

One element in the design of Browning's dramatic
monologues is, as I have said, the unfettered freedom of
the speaker's self-revelation. Another element, equally
important, is the historical background which, to answer
its purpose, must seem both real and accurate. Further,
it is often a background of special significance. Browning
loves to choose some moment of crisis, some period when
great issues hang in the balance. In *An Epistle* and *Cleon*,
the moment is one in which Christianity has just opened
upon an unbelieving world: *A Death in the Desert* is dated
a short time later. The Renaissance is one of his favourite
periods: *The Bishop orders his Tomb at St. Praxed's*, *My
Last Duchess*, *Andrea del Sarto* are all Renaissance poems,
and *A Grammarian's Funeral* is headed 'Shortly after the
revival of learning in Europe'. Even in *Bishop Blougram's
Apology*, a more or less precise date is essential to the
conception:

Had I been born three hundred years ago
They'd say, ' What's strange? Blougram of course believes;'
And, seventy years since, ' disbelieves of course'.
But now, ' He may believe; and yet, and yet
How can he?'

[1] *Ned Bratts*, 180.   [2] Stanza xxvii.

Sometimes, though not so often, Browning is equally explicit about place, heading the poems ' Rome ' or ' Ferrara ', or making it plain from the context that the scene is London, Florence, or elsewhere. The illusion of historical accuracy is necessary to the effect which he seeks to produce. But, binding himself in one way, he leaves himself free in another—the main character is either little known or wholly imaginary. Hence the detailed picture which he draws violates no familiar facts. On one occasion when he breaks this rule, namely in his portrait of Napoleon III, he secures some measure of freedom by calling the ex-Emperor ' Prince Hohenstiel-Schwangau ', but even this dialogue receives the precise and significant date, 1871.

In this scheme of producing the appearance of historical exactness, without sacrificing the poet's freedom of invention, diction plays an important part. Browning cares nothing for an atmosphere of vague romantic beauty, nothing for verbal melody or suggestion on their own account. He surveys remote lands and remote ages through a pellucid atmosphere: distance lends no enchantment to the view. The difference between him and his contemporaries is illustrated by his use of the word *argosy*. It is the historic element in this word that Browning brings out, not its vague romantic suggestiveness. The word occurs only in his play *The Return of the Druses*, where it is used four times, each time of *Venetian* ships. His scheme demands the accumulation of many small exact details of time, place, and circumstance. Hence the care bestowed on local colour, hence the frequent naturalization of foreign words, hence too the wealth of technical terms. His method is well displayed in his poem on the dying Bishop of St. Praxed's with his passion for architecture. The speaker's tastes are illustrated by the number and precision of his technical terms: ' *onion-stone* ' (' cipollino '), ' *antique-black* ' (' nero antico '), *lapis lazuli, gritstone, mortcloth, tabernacle, vizor, bas-relief, entablature, travertine.* The first seven words in this list are not used elsewhere by Browning—a proof of his careful differentiation of one poem from another. A similar effect is produced in *An Epistle* with its fitting display of medical terms: *snakestone, gum-tragacanth, sublimate* (noun), *tertian, viscid*: these words also are not used again in Browning's poetry. One wonders what other poet could have given such clear-cut reality to an imaginary letter from an Arab physician of the First Century. It is more difficult to differentiate the language of a speaker who is not presented in his professional capacity or under any one aspect. Yet Browning succeeds here also. Bishop Blougram, for instance, is revealed less as a prelate than as a cultivated man of the world. Such a man, talking rapidly and intimately, will sometimes coin a word on the spur of the moment, sometimes use a rare word which he has perhaps never thought of before. It is thus that the Bishop does in fact speak: *decrassify* here makes its first appearance not only in Browning's work but apparently in the English language as well; *entourage, demirep, eventuality, experimentalise, excitation, fictile* occur in this dialogue and nowhere else in Browning. For the poet's peculiar method, great learning was necessary, and Browning's learning is generally to be trusted, though there are a few phantom allusions, like the 'Emperor Aldabrod' of *The Heretic's Tragedy*. It is true of Browning as of Milton that to appreciate him to the full is one of the rewards of consummated scholarship. His best work is strong enough to carry off some effect of strangeness in the language. Thus *loric* was not a word before Browning used it in his Roman poem *Protus*, but it suits the context and it dispels the intervening centuries better than 'breast-plate'. It is of course not the case in poetry that the end justifies the means. The technical terms which Browning uses for a special dramatic purpose do not in his hands immediately turn into poetry, like the technical terms of Milton in the line:

Cornice, or frieze with bossy sculptures graven.

Nor can the language of the arts have the same universal appeal as the common language of men. On that ground at least a cuckoo's cry is better described as a 'twofold shout' than as a 'minor third'.[1] Opinions on the merits of the second phrase will naturally differ. For my part I cannot help liking it any more than I can help liking the 'commiserating sevenths' of *A Toccata of Galuppi's*; but that is a purely personal view.

[1] *Lovers' Quarrel*, 123.

No poetry is safe in ignoring altogether the ideal of simplicity. It is characteristic of Browning that he so seldom approaches 'the plain dignity of Biblical English. His diction is centrifugal: his restless activity impels him to avoid the norm; for him, as for Abt Vogler, the C Major of this life is a resting-place which invites sleep. Nor is he the man to use moderation. Some of his work, especially that of his later life, reads like a parody of his own method. The lines in *A Grammarian's Funeral*:

> He settled *Hoti's* business—let it be!—
> Properly based *Oun*—

produce a slight shock when first read, but, when familiar, they may give a kind of pleasure; so much can scarcely be said of:

> *Amo -as -avi -atum -are -ans*,
> Up to *-aturus*, person, tense, and mood.[1]

Nor is it clear why Count Guido Franceschini, who is not a physician, should call a pain in his shoulder-blade 'an ailing in this omoplat'.[2] On the matter of technical terms in verse no two persons can possibly feel in the same way, a fact which in itself tells against them. For my own part, I can see why Browning in his character of dramatic realist should allude to the Pope's *cheirograph*[3] in *The Ring and the Book*, that being the correct term for 'one of three forms in which the will of the Papal See is expressed in writing'. I can also see some ground for the allusion to *tarocs* (i.e. playing-cards) in Caponsacchi's autobiographical sketch.[4] But to form a nonce-word *baioc*[5] from 'bajocco', the name of a small Italian coin, is simply unfair to the reader. Browning's declared principles in diction are cosmopolitan. He is naturally amused at 'the sturdy Briton who, Ben Jonson informs us, wrote "The Life of the Emperor Anthony Pie"—whom we now acquiesce in as Antoninus Pius', but a little more insularity would have done nothing but good to Browning himself. Why, for instance, should he coin *ampollosity* from the Italian 'ampolloso' rather than *ampullosity*, from the Latin

---

[1] *The Ring and the Book*, viii. 5, 6.　　　　[2] Ibid. v. 118.
[3] Usually spelt 'chirograph'.
[4] *The Ring and the Book*, vi. 349.
[5] Ibid. v. 542. Perhaps alliteration was the motive. The line is:
'The broil o' the brazier, pays the due baioc'; *v. infra*, p. 129.

'ampullosus'?   The mere fact that he was writing a poem on Italian life is hardly reason enough.   His refusal to latinize Greek names in the traditional manner, using instead such forms as *Olumpos, Phaidra, Phoibos, Sophokles, Klutaimnestra* is a small thing in itself, but it is significant of his attitude towards English usage.   In his translation of the *Agamemnon* he aimed, as he tells us, at producing 'the very turn of each phrase in as Greek a fashion as English will bear'.   He applies this principle to his diction in *Aristophanes' Apology*, giving us such expressions as : *dikast and heliast, kordax-step, peplosed and kothorned, choinix, barbiton, exomion* and *chaunoprokt*.

V

Some features of Browning's style are, as we have seen, the result of a particular end in view; they are necessary to his original handling of the dramatic monologue.   But his language has other characteristics which must be considered in themselves, not in relation to any special purpose.   Some of these points are of grammatical rather than of critical interest ; some are blemishes which simply illustrate the weaker side of a powerful and brilliant writer; some suggest that in the obscurer parts of his nature this Victorian poet had affinities with the writers of an age very different and distant from his own.

A superficial but conspicuous feature of Browning's style is his use of the superlative termination *-est*, and less frequently the comparative termination *-er*, on occasions when it is more idiomatic to use 'most' or 'more' before the uninflected adjective or adverb.   Other Victorian writers have this habit, Carlyle in particular, and less noticeably Ruskin and Arnold.   Carlyle probably led the fashion.   In Browning the practice begins early : *Sordello*, for instance, furnishes such examples as *distinctest, complexest, ficklest, notablest* ; other poems contain *ineffablest, properest, directest, liberalest, dismalest, irreligiousest, sensitivest, heinousest, whimperingest, sagaciousest, benignantest, beauteousest*—a list which does not do much credit to Browning's ear.   Examples of the rare comparatives are : *formidabler, truelier, clearlier, richlier, promptlier, safelier*. He freely uses or forms verbal compounds of the type in which the adverb comes first instead of second, as in

normal prose usage. His favourite adverbial prefix is *out-*,
as in *outbreak, outburst, outcourse, outflash, outpick, outpour*;
another is *up-*, as in *upbear, upheave, up-patter*. He re-
sembles Carlyle in his lavish use of the prefix *be-*, whether
to form verbs like *becloud, bedaub, beflatter*, or to form
participial adjectives in the manner of Carlyle's *bediademed,
becoronetted, bemitred*. In formations of the second type
'the force of the be- is often merely rhetorical, expressing depreciation, ridicule, or raillery'.[1] In Browning are
various examples, e.g.

> Lord So-and-So—his coat *bedropt* with wax.[2]
>
> Its cobweb work, *betinseled* stitchery.[3]
>
> Fop *be-flattered*, Hunks *be-friended*, Hag *be-lovered*.[4]

The eccentricity in the style of Carlyle and Browning is
largely due to their ancestry and upbringing. Neither
had any interest in that Public School and University
English of which Thackeray and Arnold, each in his own
way, are masters. Browning had a fine skill in the use
of colloquial language, but the forms of it he knew
best were those which are least cramped by insularity or
class-consciousness. He brilliantly imitates the after-
dinner conversation of a Roman Catholic Bishop; with an
Anglican he would not have succeeded so well. That he
lived long out of touch with England is plain from his
irregular or old-fashioned accentuation of certain words.
I have noticed the following examples in *Aristophanes'
Apology*: consúmmating, panégyric, demónstrated, cón-
tumély ('Whatever contumely fouls the mouth'). In *The
Ring and the Book* are: súbjacent, promúlgate, revénue,[5]
bastárd, marítal, and many more are certainly to be found.

VI

Though Browning sometimes wrote as an artist sub-
duing his wayward impulses to the end in view, his unruly
passion for verbal eccentricity was always ready to burst
out. Some of his subjects were of a nature to impose

---

[1] *O.E.D.*   [2] *Bishop Blougram's Apology.*
[3] *Red Cotton Night-Cap Country*, iii. 272.
[4] *Pietro of Albano*, 215.
[5] The usual accentuation in Shakespeare, and not uncommon in later
verse.

little restraint upon him, and there were periods of his
life when the passion for oddity was especially violent.
The love of verbal freaks in a great master of English is
a curious phenomenon, and its causes are complex.   There
was in Browning something of the antinomian, much of
the humorist, much of the satirist, and scarcely anything
of the scholar's conventional restraint.   His family traditions were nonconformist; his education was learned but
irregular.   In his early manhood he travelled in Russia,
and his married life was spent mostly in Italy.   He had
a close affinity with the spirit of the Renaissance and
sometimes reminds us of one of its cosmopolitan scholars,
yet England inspires him with affection and pride, and
there is no doubt of his patriotism.   A more complex
character does not exist among our greater writers.   If to
all this is added the recollection that he was an impulsive
writer who believed that the first fine careless rapture
could never be recovered, that he did not much polish
what he had once written but 'had a vigorous way of
writing finis at the end of his poems',[1] it will not be
surprising if certain qualities of his style present the critic
with a peculiarly difficult problem.

The purpose of Browning's rare words is often clear
enough.   Many in *Sordello*, for instance, have the same
object as those in the best poems of *Men and Women*:
they contribute to the local or historical colour.   But one
wonders why he so often chooses the unfamiliar form of
a word which is itself sufficiently unfamiliar; for Browning is clearly not a Milton or a Tennyson to weigh
the musical value of a single letter.   Why, for instance,
in *Sordello*, should he write *valvassor* for 'vavasour',
truchman for 'dragoman', *plectre* for 'plectrum', *trifoly*
for 'trefoil', *orpine* for 'orpiment'?   Possibly the pre-
Raphaelites had an inkling of the answer, for some of
these words have the medieval flavour which they liked,
and Browning's early work helped to form their style.
Throughout his career Browning had a taste for obscure
and obsolete words and forms of words.   For 'frantic' he
will write *frenetic*; for 'restive', *restif*; for 'swart', *swarth*;
for 'snigger', *snicker*; for 'spit', *spawl*; for 'canter' or
'curvet', *tittup*.   It is just like him to introduce the word

---

[1] H. H. Hatcher, *The Versification of Robert Browning*.

cue-owl, a word used by himself and Mrs. Browning, but unknown, it seems, to the world at large. The strain which he puts on the use of rare words sometimes amounts to inaccuracy. In one of his poems, *catafalk*, which properly means 'a stage or platform erected to receive a coffin', is used for 'a kind of open hearse or funeral car'; in the same poem *encolure*, a French word for 'the neck of an animal' is used to mean 'the mane' (of a horse). Browning frequently forms or uses participles analogous to Milton's *increate* from 'increatus', a practice common among writers of the sixteenth and early seventeenth centuries. Examples are: *exenterate, miscreate, saturate, contaminate, extravasate, unimplicate, undesecrate, consecrate, decollate, excommunicate, affiliate*, to which may be added *attent* from 'attentus', and *porporate* from the Italian 'porporato'. Some of Browning's Latinisms seem to belong to the age of Burton or Browne rather than to the nineteenth century: for instance *benefic, crepitant, strepitant, mollitious*. The words in these last two lists, though queer and crabbed, at least bear the marks of scholarship, but occasionally Browning, like Spenser, incurs the reproach of 'writing no language'. There is, for example, his hybrid *ombrifuge* irregularly formed from ὄμβρος and -fuge, but this is not an extreme instance. Nor is his erroneous use of *lure* for 'a trap or snare': here at least he is in company with others, including Disraeli. But in some of his verbal escapades he is apparently companionless. I do not suppose any other writer has adopted his *gadge*, which, the *Oxford Dictionary* informs us, is 'used by Browning as the name of some instrument of torture'; nor has much further use been found either for *grudgment*, which is his rhyme for 'judgment', or for *stomp*, which is 'used by Browning (to obtain a rime) for *stump* or *stamp*'.[1]

VII

Like most English poets, Browning frequently forms compound words, both nouns and adjectives. A number

---

[1] Browning's rhymes, as such, do not come within the scope of this paper. His diction is, I think, bolder and more experimental in his blank verse than in his rhyming verse. But sometimes he certainly uses a word which he would not have thought of otherwise, for the sake of a rhyme, e.g. manage—*tannage* (*Flight of the Duchess*).

of his compounds are neat and beautiful in the manner
of Tennyson; others show characteristic boldness or ex-
travagance. He is fond of cumulative effects which are
more energetic than euphonious: e.g. 'That black-eyed
brown-skinned country-flavoured wench'; 'smooth-man-
nered soft-speeched sleek-cheeked visitor'. Many of his
compounds contain three or more elements: e.g. 'bugle-
bright-blackness', 'middle-age-manners-adapter', 'linden-
flower-time', 'hare-slice-and-peasoup-season', 'bugaboo-
and-baby-work', and—most extravagant of all—'monstr'-
inform'-ingens-horrend-ous'.[1] He is more effective when
he shows more restraint, as in 'the quiet-coloured end
of evening', 'an old pale-swathed majesty'. As I have
pointed out elsewhere,[2] his use of the asyntactic compound epithet e.g. '*green-flesh* melons' anticipates some of
the experiments of G. M. Hopkins.

Browning liked the vigorous effect of accumulated
epithets; he also liked the emphasis of alliteration. In
poems of his middle period, it is not uncommon to meet
these two effects in combination: for instance in Fra
Lippo Lippi's description of himself in his own painting,

Mazed, motionless, and moon-struck,

and in the account which Karshish gives of his meeting
with Lazarus:

Out there came
A moon made like a face with certain spots
Multiform, manifold, and menacing.

Browning's taste for alliteration grew with years; and in
some of his later work, when he wrote with a flowing pen
and gave free play to his satirical mood, an effect is produced which is curious in itself and interesting to students
of our early poetry. From the time of *The Ring and the
Book* onwards, one meets with line after line, passage after
passage, in which alliteration enforces the emphasis on
certain key-words with remarkable vigour. I will quote
a few examples from the large number which I have
noticed:

[1] *Æneid*, iii. 658: monstrum horrendum, informe, ingens, cui lumen
ademptum.   Browning's compound occurs in *Waring*, iv.
[2] *S.P.E. Tract XLIX.*

*P*roves a *p*lague-*p*rodigy to God and man.[1]
*L*ook at my *l*awyers, *l*acked they grace of *l*aw,
*L*atin or *l*ogic?[2]

Out with you! *T*rundle, log!
If you cannot *t*ramp and *t*rudge like a man, *t*ry all-fours like a
   dog![3]

*fl*at thus I lie nor *fl*inch!
O God, the *f*eel of the *f*ang *f*urrowing my shoulder!—see!
It *g*rinds—it *g*rates the bone.[4]

In these passages alliteration seems to be struggling to
become the master-principle of the metre as it was in our
ancient poetry, and when one meets a succession of lines
like the following, one feels that the spirit and manner of
a long-forgotten past have mysteriously revived in this
mid-Victorian writer:

I tried chaff, *f*ound I *f*amished on such *f*are,
So *m*ade this *m*ad rush at the *m*ill-house door,
Buried my head up to the ears in dew,
*B*rowsed on the *b*est: for which you *b*rain me, Sirs![5]

Alliteration has played a part in the verse of many English
poets since the Elizabethan age, but for a parallel to this
regular use of it upon three stressed words in the line we
must go back to the alliterative poets before Wyatt and
Surrey.   In the tone of the passages which I have quoted,
we hear something of the voice of Langland: he, like
Browning, was a poet of headlong energy and unvarnished
speech.   But, for my own part, I am reminded even more
clearly of the West Midland author of *Patience*, that poet
of many moods, the tender, the humorous, the denunciatory.   Surely there is something remarkably like certain
phases of Browning's style in the abuse which is showered
on Jonah by the sailors in the ship bound for Tarshish:

What þe deuel hatȝ þou don, doted wrech!
What seches þou on see, synful schrewe,
With þy lastes so luþer to lose vus vchone?
Hatȝ þou, gome, no gouernour ne god on to calle,
Þat þou þus slydes on slepe when þou slayn worþes?[6]

This parallel is almost certainly due to the development
of a natural tendency in Browning's style, and not to any

---

[1] *The Ring and the Book*, v. 664.   [2] Ibid. xi. 1757-8.
[3] *Halbert and Hob.*   [4] *Ivàn Ivànovitch.*
[5] *The Ring and the Book*, xi. 1482-5.   [6] *Patience*, ii. 196-200.

study of early English verse. That a modern poet should revert, though but for a moment, to the style of so remote an age, is surely a curious fact in the history of style.

I have dwelt freely on what I presume to call the 'faults' of Browning's diction, yet it is clear that he was a great though irregular master of English. His influence on the language has been small in proportion to his powers. As we have seen, he is possibly the inventor of the word *artistry*, and a few of his phrases are current, e.g. 'the first fine careless rapture', 'the little more, and how much it is! And the little less, and what worlds away'; but his contribution to the language is much smaller than Tennyson's. In his lifetime, the influence of his style was not wide, but it was apparent in the work of two or three outstanding men. The pre-Raphaelites caught something of the spirit of his early style. It is possible that D. G. Rossetti learned from Browning his idiom of the possessive noun + metaphor, e.g. 'her neck's rose-misted marble' (Browning), 'her eyes' o'erhanging heaven' (Rossetti). Certain features in the style of G. M. Hopkins are evidently borrowed from Browning, e.g. the accumulation of compound epithets, the asyntactic compound epithet (in which Hopkins is bolder than his master) and perhaps the use of emphatic monosyllables in a compact series. Browning's most profitable example to later poets lay in his use of colloquial English for the impassioned lyric. As G. K. Chesterton excellently puts it: 'He substituted the street with the green blind for the faded garden of Watteau, and the "blue spirt of a lighted match" for the monotony of the evening star.' In this respect Hardy is Browning's disciple, and from Hardy the example has spread far and wide into modern verse. That Browning's dramatic monologues have been little imitated is natural, for each piece has its distinct style, and to write a series of such poems would demand a combination of powers such as Browning alone possessed. Few writers have ever paid less regard to critics; he almost seems, like the fourteenth-century poets with whom I have compared him, to belong to a pre-critical age. 'Tennyson', he noted, 'reads the Quarterly and does as they bid him with the most solemn face in the world—out goes this, in goes that, all is changed and ranged. Oh me!' Browning

could not have been what he was without his sturdy in-
dependence; yet his best admirers cannot help wishing
that he had heeded—if not the criticism of living men—
at least the silent and searching criticism which is opera-
tive in the spirit of the English language.

ARNOLD

I

THIS Essay, which is a chapter in the history of English poetic style, would be incomplete without a section on Matthew Arnold. Though younger than Tennyson and Browning, he died before either, so that he is by his dates a mid-Victorian poet. He has the amplitude of mind and the seriousness of outlook which the best men of his generation possessed: it may be, indeed, that in these respects he surpassed his contemporaries. He is untouched by the aestheticism of the later Victorian age: poetry is to him a 'criticism of life'. Like Wordsworth he strives to bring his poetic style as nearly as possible into line with 'the real language of men'; he dislikes any conscious attempt to widen the gap between prose and poetry. His diction is more vital than Swinburne's, which is too literary, more real than Morris's, which is too archaic. So much at least may be said in Arnold's favour; yet it must be admitted that, in point of language, he is less interesting than either Tennyson or Browning. The style of these two writers is, at all events, strongly individual: Arnold's has much less character, it is individual only in certain places. The very faults of Tennyson and Browning are interesting, and bring us by a direct route to the most important problems of poetic expression. Arnold's faults are largely negative, and therefore have little significance for the critic. It should be added, however, that Arnold's diction is not, like Tennyson's, his strong point; further, that he wrote many poems and passages in a style beautiful enough to satisfy the severest critic.

Unlike Tennyson and Browning, Arnold was a professional critic, and he rated the importance of criticism very high. He wrote much on style, and one of his books, *On Translating Homer*, is concerned entirely with metre and diction. He also wished to establish a connexion between his criticism and his poetry: his *Poems* of 1853, and his tragedy *Merope*, are both introduced by elaborate Prefaces. Yet for our immediate purpose, Arnold's criticism is comparatively unimportant. He was a poet before he was a critic, and his work in those two capacities is really quite distinct. Sir Walter Raleigh maintains—justly, in my opinion—that Arnold was not well qualified to be a critic of English literature. 'There is no evidence', he writes, 'that he ever understood the English character'; and again, 'In a certain sense, Matthew Arnold's attitude to English literature was that of a foreigner.' But he is no foreigner in his poetry, and though his affection for England may not appear in his criticism, it penetrates his verse, and has made him one of the best poets of the English landscape. Reference to his criticism will be made from time to time in this study, but his poetry will be treated as virtually an independent subject.

Though Arnold was in some senses an inheritor of the Romantic tradition, his relations with it were far less intimate than those of Tennyson and Browning. He was, in fact, consciously on his guard against its dangers. He underwent no youthful enthusiasm for its youthful poets. He did not, like Tennyson, imbibe the spirit of Keats in his early manhood; he never had Browning's adolescent adoration of Shelley. The poet of that generation whom he knew best and admired most was Wordsworth, the master of the pure style; Byron he also admired, but with a clear sense of his faults. The qualities which Arnold esteemed in poetry were simplicity, restraint, austerity; how far this taste was innate, how far acquired, it is impossible to say; but it is evident that his mind was more closely moulded by formal education than the mind of Tennyson or Browning. Some time for vagrant studies was probably left by the classical curriculum in the Rugby of Arnold's day, but there was certainly less freedom there for the 'growth of a poet's mind' than at Hawkshead, or even at Louth or Camberwell. In later life, Arnold acquired many new tastes of his own, but he remained faithful to the masters of whom his father most approved. Homer was to him always the infallible poet; of the Bible he remained an unwearied reader, nor did he ever fail in his admiration for Wordsworth. It was an invigorating education that Arnold received, but there was no escape from its influence, and it did much to determine the character of his poetry for good or ill.

II

A poet's choice of measures is always significant. The metres and rhyme-schemes of Arnold are mostly of the simple kind. He wrote a number of sonnets rhymed after the Petrarchan model, but his measures are usually much less exacting. His favourite forms are: blank verse (with far less artistry than Tennyson's), quatrains with alternate rhymes, six-lined stanzas of quatrain and couplet, and various forms of irregular verse, usually with easy rhyming-schemes, sometimes with no rhyme at all. Even in the stanza used in *The Scholar Gipsy* and *Thyrsis*, no end-word is rhymed more than once. As the measures are, so is the diction: it is sparingly adorned, and often austere. His early style is experimental, but there is a clear preference for simplicity. There is not much ornament in his prize-poem, *Cromwell* (1843). His next volume, *The Strayed Reveller, and Other Poems* (1849) contains *Mycerinus*, a poem which Arnold often reprinted. Its style is modelled on that of Wordsworth's *Laodamia*, and though it falls far short of its original in concentrated strength, it has something of the same austerity, and something of the same Latinized diction. The reflective mood which is evident in the volume of 1849 becomes more pronounced in that of 1852, and to express it Arnold employs a style which he might have described in Dryden's lines on the heroic couplet:

> This unpolished, rugged verse I chose
> As fittest for discourse, and nearest prose.

Not only is Arnold's reflective verse often as near to prose as poetry can be, but there are passages in it which vividly recall the seventeenth-century manner. The following stanza, for instance, is almost exactly in a style used by Dryden and Marvell:

> And we, whose ways were unlike here,
> May then more neighbouring courses ply;
> May to each other be brought near,
> And greet across infinity.[1]

This note is rare in Arnold, but his reflective style shows a marked tendency to epigrammatic antithesis. He is fond of a sententious form of words like:

[1] *A Farewell*, 73–6.

> Neither made man too much a God,
> Nor God too much a man.[1]

This kind of pointed expression is natural in the poetry which lies nearest to prose. There are poets with whom Arnold has a deeper affinity, but on the critical side of his nature he has much in common with Dryden. They have the same taste for simplicity, the same suspicion of false ornament.

Arnold said of Wordsworth 'he has no style'. Something of the weakness which these words are meant to indicate is evident in Arnold's own work. His principle of composition seems to have been that of Horace:

> Cui lecta potenter erit res,
> Nec facundia deseret hunc, nec lucidus ordo.

There were a number of ' res' which inspired Arnold with poetic eloquence; there were others which had not this power, and it is in writing of them that he betrays the lack of an habitual sustaining style. This point I will illustrate shortly: a minor but connected matter is his frequent disregard of verbal neatness. Arnold is not strong in the lesser virtues of style. Few good poets since the time of Pope have taken so little trouble to avoid the fault of hiatus. Phrases like ' *the ills* we ought to bear ', ' the fight that crown'd *thy ills* ', pardonable enough if exceptional, are in Arnold extremely common. Another characteristic, also tending to the slowness of his verse, is his practice of giving the value of two syllables to words like *spasm*,[2] *choir*, *fire*, *towards*, *flower*, *tired*. A more serious fault is his failure to produce ' that subtle heightening and change ' which are required for a ' genuine poetic style '.[3] It is not rare to meet in his poems passages which read like an excerpt from one of his essays cast loosely into the form of verse. In the following lines, for instance, though the value of the reflection is undeniable, the effect of poetry is bareiy attained, and the last line is completely prosaic:

[1] *Obermann*, 59, 60. Similar passages are: ll. 71–2; 95–6 ibid.; *On the Rhine*, 19, 20; *Stanzas from the Grande Chartreuse*, 159, 160.
[2] Contrast, e.g. Milton, *P.L.* xi. 481: All maladies Of ghastly spasm, or racking torture, qualms, &c.
[3] Preface to ' Poems of Wordsworth, chosen and edited by Matthew Arnold '.

And many a man in his own breast then delves,
But deep enough, alas, none ever mines:
And we have been on many thousand lines,
And we have shown on each talent and power,
But hardly have we, for one little hour,
Been on our own line, have we been ourselves.[1]

Arnold's best work is free from passages like this, but when
his energy flags he is apt to lapse into a bathos like that
for which Wordsworth has been so much blamed, the only
difference being that Wordsworth's bathos is one of plati-
tude or rustic simplicity, while Arnold keeps his literary
manner.   Lines like:

By other rules than are in vogue to-day (*Empedocles on Etna*) ;

passages like:

> The other, maturer in fame,
> Earning, she too, her praise
> First in Fiction, had since
> Widen'd her sweep, and survey'd
> History, Politics, Mind (*Haworth Churchyard*),

clearly belong to the prosaic rather than to the poetic
criticism of life.   Occasionally Arnold does come very near
to the bald literalness of Wordsworth's weaker moments.
Had such a line as this one in *Balder Dead*—

> Nine days he took to go, two to return—

occurred in *The Prelude* or *The Excursion*, it would have
been held up to ridicule often enough.   Some of the poems,
like *Revolutions*, stand solely on their thought, but there
are times when even a purely intellectual effect is spoilt by
a stanza so utterly second-rate as:

> But so many books thou readest,
> But so many schemes thou breedest,
> But so many wishes feedest,
>   That thy poor head almost turns.[2]

Arnold's habit of using italics is unfortunate: it is a practice associated with the dogmatism of the teacher, and we
suspect poetry which has designs upon us.

In his Lectures on translating Homer, Arnold has much
to say on the failure to render the grand simplicity of
Homer's style.   He condemns all that is fanciful, eccentric,

---

[1] *The Buried Life*, 55–60.   [2] *The Second Best*, 5–8.

quaint, or rustic. Discussing a passage in Newman's version, he remarks that 'as a matter of diction "O gentle friend", "eld", "in sooth", "liefly", "advance", "man-ennobling", "sith", "any-gait", and "sly of foot" are all bad', but he modifies the effect of this by saying later: 'Of all the words which, placed where Mr. Newman places them, I have called bad words, every one may be excellent in some other place.' Arnold, for his own part, generally follows the safe advice of Quintilian: 'Consuetudo certissima linguae magistra', though one wonders, in passing, whether there is anything 'quainter' in Newman than the phrase 'sustains the wise, the foolish *elf*',[1] in which the last word is a synonym for 'man' chosen as a rhyme to 'himself'. Still, it is true that Arnold uses comparatively few words or forms of words of the so-called 'poetic' or archaic kind. Among the examples which occur are *frith* (firth), *gulph, sheen, marges, prore, wots, main* (sea), *steeds, eterne, drear, amain, morns, eves, teen, wroth, frore*. I conjecture that several of these were permitted as being nearer to their classical equivalents than the usual forms. Thus *marge* is nearer to 'margo' than 'margin'; *prore* to 'prora' than 'prow'; *eterne* to 'æternus' than 'eternal'. *Frith* is really a metathetic form of 'firth', but it was commonly supposed to be allied to 'fretum' in Arnold's time.

Verbal reminiscences from classical authors are common in Arnold's poetry, and have been the subject of various criticisms. One writer[2] points out some of the Homeric parallels: 'the feeble shadowy tribes of Hell' and ἀμενηνὰ κάρηνα; 'twittering ghosts' and τετριγυῖα ψυχὴ; 'And is alone not dipt in Ocean's stream' and οἴη δ'ἄμμορός ἐστι λοετρῶν 'Ωκεανοῖο; 'long-necked cranes' and γεράνων . . . δουλιχοδείρων. Arnold has been blamed for treating the theme of *Sohrab and Rustum*, which is Persian, and that of *Balder Dead*, which is Norse, so much in the classical manner. Stopford Brooke, for instance, considers that 'the Homeric tradition is out of place in *Sohrab and Rustum*' and calls *Balder Dead* 'almost absurdly Homerized'. I agree that in execution neither poem is wholly satisfactory, but these criticisms make the matter appear simpler

---

[1] *Empedocles on Etna*, I. ii. 306.
[2] R. E. C. Houghton in *The Influence of the Classics on the Poetry of Matthew Arnold*.

than it really is. It cannot be maintained that Homeric echoes are only allowable in poems on a Greek theme: no one objects to the classicism in *Paradise Lost*. The point, rather, is that in *Sohrab and Rustum* and *Balder Dead* Arnold is not always in his natural element: parts are spontaneous, parts are laboured. In plain narrative Arnold is not like Homer; rather he is like Virgil, without Virgil's unfailing charm of style. What is lacking in a passage like the following—and it fairly represents the style in large portions of both poems—is the touch of verbal distinction which a Virgil or a Tennyson would have given it:

> The table stood beside him, charg'd with food;
> A side of roasted sheep, and cakes of bread,
> And dark green melons.[1]

Here, as in many other places, there is none of 'that subtle heightening and change' required for a 'genuine poetic style'. But when Arnold writes

> and from his limbs
> Unwillingly the spirit fled away,
> Regretting the warm mansion which it left,
> And youth and bloom, and this delightful world,[2]

his feelings inspire a perfectly satisfying rhythm and diction: the passage is like one of those finer passages in Virgil which would still be poetic without the Virgilian manner. Arnold's good sense as a critic prevents him from spoiling the stories which he has to tell, but it is in the atmosphere, the background, the similes, and above all in the reflective and elegiac passages that he proves himself a poet; in these he moves the reader because he is deeply moved himself. Had the author of *The Scholar Gipsy*, who voices so well 'the sick fatigue, the languid doubt' of his own day, been able also to recapture some tones of the epic voice which he admired so much in Homer, he would have been the greatest poet of his generation. But this width of inspiration Arnold did not possess. Some half-dozen notes he can strike effectively; attempting more, he is evidently at a loss. He feels deeply as poet and scholar the beauty of classical myths and of the Oxford landscape; he is a stoic recommending moderate hopes,

[1] *Sohrab and Rustum*, 197-9.   [2] Ibid. 853-6.

'close-lipp'd patience' and fidelity to the inward light; he knows the fickleness of joy and the rarity of peace, and clings all the more stedfastly to the things which endure, 'what will be for ever; what was from of old.' On these themes he always finds the right tone and the right words, and when he combines them in a single poem, he is one of the best of our elegiac poets.

III

A study of Arnold's characteristic words reveals both his strength as a poet and also his limitations. Inward austerity, as he tells us in a sonnet,[1] does not prevent the work of a poet from attaining outward radiance, and in Arnold's best poems, however severely planned, there is much beautiful diction. At the same time he appears, even in the comparatively small volume of his published verse, to be putting a strain upon his invention, for felicitous expressions in one piece are sometimes almost exactly repeated in another.

The repetition of words in poetry may be a sign of resource, or it may be a sign of limitation. I have shown elsewhere with what variety of effect Shakespeare uses the verb *gild*:[2] in some half-dozen contexts it produces the effect of as many different words. On the other hand, the repeated use of the adjective *dull* in some of Crabbe's verse is simply monotonous: the repetition is perhaps intentional, but the effect is like the continual striking of a single note. Arnold's work provides instances of both these kinds of repetition. One of his favourite epithets is *white*. This word he uses in various contexts, often with that touch of unexpectedness which is the life of poetic language: '*white* sleeping town', '*white* evening-star', '*whitening* hedges', '*white*-blossom'd trees'. These phrases are vivid and fresh. But when we come to '*white* fog', 'cold *white* mist', '*white* rolling vapours', '*white* peaks', '*white* snows', the epithet begins to lose its force by familiarity. It was a happy thought to substitute *blanch'd* for *white*, and Arnold forms the beautiful compound epithet *moon-blanch'd*: but even this word is used twice, once with 'green' and once

[1] *Austerity of Poetry*, 12–14.
[2] *Some Kinds of Poetic Diction* (Essays and Studies of the English Association, vol. xv).

with 'street'. In *Thyrsis*—a poem in which one is loath to find any fault—the epithet *pale* occurs three times in fifteen lines. Some of the repeated words do not lend themselves to differentiation. In the following phrases, for instance, '*high* unfrequented mountain spots', '*high* mountain pastures', '*high* the mountain-tops', 'the *high* mountain platforms', '*high*-pasturing kine' the same note is struck each time, though it is a characteristic note which one enjoys and respects. Other words in Arnold are also characteristic, e.g. *austere* and the much-iterated *calm*. He is noticeably apt to repeat his felicities. For example, 'blue *Midland waters*' in *The Scholar Gipsy* is an attractive phrase for the Mediterranean, but in *A Southern Night* we also come across 'this *Midland* deep'; the pleasant simplicity of 'the lights come out' in a description of the scattered farms near Oxford at evening [1] reappears verbatim in the lines on an autumn evening at Rugby.[2]

A further examination of Arnold's diction, in its various phases, confirms these general impressions. Compound epithets are often characteristic of their author, and Arnold's follow this rule. In one group there are many traces of unconscious autobiography. The following list is very suggestive of their author's inner life: *heart-wearying, heart-wasting, care-fill'd, clearest-soul'd, high-soul'd, even-balanc'd* (soul); and the stoical self-discipline of Arnold's philosophy is indicated in the large number of formations in which *self-* is the first element: e.g. *self-sufficing, self-helping, self-ordain'd, self-govern'd, self-master'd*, and the group of four in the sonnet 'Shakespeare': *self-school'd, self-scann'd, self-honour'd, self-secure*. Descriptive compound epithets are fairly numerous in Arnold's verse; they are one of the beauties of his two best poems, and no reader of *The Scholar Gipsy* and *Thrysis* can have missed their effect in phrases like '*air-swept* lindens'; 'warm *green-muffled* Cumner hills'; '*frail-leaf'd*, white anemone'; 'dark *red-fruited* yew-tree's shade'; '*gold-dusted* snapdragon'. It is also in descriptive phrases that Arnold's somewhat rare use of metaphor appears most memorably: 'white anemonies *Starr'd* the cool turf';[3] (some rich hyacinth) 'a fragrant *tower* of purple bloom';[4] (of an

---

[1] *Thyrsis*, 164.   [2] *Rugby Chapel*, 8.
[3] *Tristram and Iseult*, iii. 207–8.   [4] *Sohrab and Rustum*, 637.

eagle) 'never more Shall the lake *glass* her, flying over it'; [1]
' where the nich'd snow-bed *sprays* down Its powdery fall'; [2]
'And from the boughs the snowloads *shuffle* down'; [3] 'Soon
will the high Midsummer *pomps* come on'; [4] 'The *coronals*
of that forgotten time.' [5]   Like Browning and other poets,
Arnold shows a preference for particular affixes in forming compound verbs and participial adjectives: perhaps it
is characteristic of him to prefer the negative ones, the
prefixes *un-* (or *in-*), and the suffix *-less*.   Some negative
compounds, new or old, are used by him with remarkable
energy.   *The Scholar Gipsy* furnishes two examples in the
vigorous lines :

> Still nursing the *unconquerable* hope,
>   Still clutching the *inviolable* shade,

and *Thrysis* supplies two more in the line:

> The *morningless* and *unawakening* sleep.

In descriptive use, negatives occur in '*unwrinkled* Rhine', [6]
'The *unplumb'd*, salt, estranging sea', [7] 'the west *unflushes*', [8]
and in the beautiful phrase '*uncrumpling* fern'. [9]   Arnold's
sense of the impassivity of Nature is forcibly expressed in
the negative epithets of the lines:

> Over the *unallied unopening* earth,
>   Over the *unrecognizing* sea. [10]

Another prefix for which he shows a preference is *en-*, as
in *enisled, enclasping, engarlanded, enkerchief'd*.   Of verbal
reminiscences from other English poets there is comparatively little in Arnold's work.   Critics have named Wordsworth as his principal English model, and Wordsworth is
not a poet whose influence is traceable in the details of
style.   A close inspection of Arnold's language brings to
light a few passages in which Wordsworth's phrasing has
evidently been remembered.   The style of *Mycerinus*, as
I have already mentioned, shows a general resemblance to
that of *Laodamia*.   There is a description of pine-trees in
the poem called *A Dream* :

> the morning sun,
> On the wet *umbrage* of their glossy tops,
> On the red *pinings* of their forest floor,
> Drew a warm scent abroad,

[1] *Sohrab and Rustum*, 570.   [2] *Parting*, 49–50.
[3] *Balder Dead*, 111, 319.   [4] *Thyrsis*, 62.   [5] Ibid. 117.
[6] *On the Rhine*, 12.   [7] *To Marguerite* (1852), 24.
[8] *Thyrsis*, 163.   [9] Ibid. 74.   [10] *Empedocles on Etna*, ii. 360–1.

in which two words are obviously echoed from 'the pining umbrage' of Wordsworth's *Yew-trees*. In a passage from *Sohrab and Rustum*:

> For he remember'd his own early youth,
> And all its bounding rapture,

the second line looks like a composite of 'I bounded o'er the mountains' and 'all its dizzy raptures' (ll. 68 and 85 of *Lines composed a few miles above Tintern Abbey*). Another possible reminiscence of the same poet is the opening sentence of *The River*, 'Still glides the stream', which is identical with the first part of line 5 of the sonnet *After-Thought*. Here and there are echoes from other writers. For instance, 'its *weary, unprofitable* length '[1] is obviously Shakespearian, and Arnold's use in description of *wailful*, *moss'd* (walnut-trees), and *summer eves*, all of which are characteristic of Keats and occur in his *Autumn*, may be due to reminiscence of that poem. It is natural that so sedulous a reader of the Bible as Arnold was should show signs of its influence in his style, and it is not difficult to find examples: e.g. 'seed-time and harvest',[2] 'We bear the burden and the heat Of the long day.'[3]

Taken as a whole, Arnold's style is very unequal, and though he revised details of expression in successive editions of his poems, he was at heart much more concerned with the general plan of a work than with its execution. The mannerisms of his prose style have often been mentioned, and his poetic style has mannerisms which are not less conspicuous. Perhaps the most striking of these is the excessive use of lines consisting of three epithets or three nouns (e.g. Zealous, beneficent, firm; History, Politics, Mind). In *Rugby Chapel*, a poem of 208 lines, there are five examples of this type of line, viz. ll. 10, 43, 139, 158, 160. This mannerism occurs principally in the short-lined blank verse which is one of Arnold's favourite metres.

I have already alluded to the strong vein of reflective criticism which runs through Arnold's poetry, giving it a resemblance to that of Dryden. How successfully he wrote in this style is proved by the excellence of his quotable lines, for instance: 'Who saw life steadily, and

---

[1] *The Youth of Man*, 110.   [2] *Empedocles on Etna*, ii. 254.
[3] *Morality*, 9–10.

saw it whole ';[1] 'France, fam'd in all great arts, in none supreme ';[2] 'The pageant of his bleeding heart'[3] (of Byron). But the poetry of the Victorian Age was the offspring of the Romantic Movement, 'a great movement of feeling', as Arnold calls it, not 'a great movement of mind'. He belonged to his age, and his deepest poetic impulse was an emotional one. Fundamentally he is an elegiac poet. The feeling from which nearly all his best work springs is summed up in the lines:

> Nature is fresh as of old,
> Is lovely : a mortal is dead.

It is the symbolization of this contrast in alternate speeches in the second act of *Empedocles on Etna* that makes that part of the poem so immeasurably finer than the first act, with its monotonous exposition of an austere philosophy. Arnold needed a complex theme to unlock the full treasury of his language. That he had such a theme in *The Scholar Gipsy* and *Thyrsis* is the reason why those two works are his best poems. There he could express to the full the contrast between his love of the Oxford landscape and his delight in the poetry of the ancient world on the one hand, and his sense of the unrest and distraction of his own age on the other. Together, these themes drew forth the full passion and beauty of his poetic voice.

It is not my task to determine the full critical significance of the conclusions which have been reached in this survey. It is clear, however, that any poetry which is widely read must leave some mark on the language in which it is written. Of the three poets who have been discussed, Tennyson's influence was far greater than that of his two contemporaries. Browning, it is true, anticipated some of the experiments of later verse, but no change in taste will ever make him popular in proportion to his intellectual vigour: the idiosyncrasies of his style will always form too great an obstacle. Tennyson's popularity, no doubt, is chiefly a thing of the past, but his influence is a historical fact of much significance, and for that reason he will always have a special interest for those philologists who

---

[1] *To a Friend.*   [2] *To a Republican Friend.*
[3] *Stanzas from the Grande Chartreuse.*

recognize the relation between language and imaginative literature. As Poet Laureate, Tennyson belonged to a succession of writers many of whom performed great services to their native tongue, and English is not less indebted to him than it is to Dryden, to Wordsworth, or to Bridges. Tennyson's faults, and in particular his over-attention to the minuter graces, fade into insignificance beside his command of a splendid vocabulary to which his many-sided talent continually gave new life. His example contributed in a hundred ways towards producing that high standard in the use of language shown by the later Victorians both in their verse and in their prose. By sympathy and interest he even had some contact with the contemporary advances in philology. He was a poet whose developing art was happily identified with the best interests of his native tongue. Without Shakespeare's sovereign mastery over words or Milton's power of impressing the stamp of his mind upon them, he rendered the language a high service by helping both to conserve and to refine it.